QUIET & BADASS

VISIONARY WOMEN EMBRACING THEIR UNIQUENESS TO CREATE EPIC IMPACT

INTROVERT, SHE WROTE PUBLISHING

Disclaimer and Content Warning

The publisher takes no legal responsibility for the details inside the stories of this book. The words and opinions are the authors' own, and the memories they describe are their lived experiences. Some of the stories contained within may be disturbing for some readers, as they explore themes related to alcohol consumption, domestic abuse and/or sexual trauma, eating disorders, suicide attempts and mental health concerns. Readers are advised to seek professional or medical assistance as necessary.

Contents

INTRODUCTION

The idea for this book came to me as I sat at a cafe table on a crisp March afternoon in South Lake Tahoe, California. It was my 40th birthday, and I had just made the decision that forty and beyond would be epic. Epic for me and for anyone who wanted to come along with me for the ride.

Each of us has our own uniquely designed personalities created and shaped by our DNA and life experiences, but we aren't always celebrated for it. Often we are misunderstood, underestimated, counted out, or flat-out rejected. We feel we have no choice but to hide, fix, or change who we are in order to be accepted.

As an Introvert, I have experienced life wondering if I would always have to wear an extroverted mask and be someone I wasn't in order to be accepted and successful. Would I always have to have two different versions of myself?

Some of us are quiet naturally, some by design, and some out of survival. The common thread that connects the quiet ones is the adversity that we've stared in the eyes and our triumphant response. Our responses have provided us with strength, courage, and a burning desire to help others with our gifts.

The concept for this book was so clear. But what would the title be?

As I sat there looking up at the enchanting snow-capped Sierra Nevada Mountains, I took in the beauty and asked myself:

How would I describe women who, despite adversity, embrace their authenticity and just freaking own it?

Badass. They're Badass!

And so it was... Quiet and Badass.

Each contributor in this book has entertained the lonely fear of never belonging, of never being chosen, or of never living up to expectations. Yet, each of them is thriving as their authentic self. I can tell you from my own experience that things get really good once you shed the layers of expectations you've collected throughout your life.

Once you wholeheartedly accept who you are at the core, you can fully step into all you came here to be.

If you have experienced, or are currently experiencing, this journey you will find comfort and inspiration throughout these pages to become unapologetically you.

May this book be a gift of comfort, courage, and inspiration for you to thrive as your most authentic and unapologetic self.

Here's to unlocking and rockin' your Inner Badass.

Xo Jenny Alberti

EXCLUSIVE BOOK BONUSES

To download, scan the QR code, or visit:

https://sqr.co/qab-book-bonus

LAURA RINNANKOSKI

UNSTOPPABLE CITIZEN OF THE WORLD

The Choices of Our Lives

When I think of the word *Badass*, I conjure the image of a person who has been through a lot in life, but has never given up. To me, a *Badass* makes the conscious choice to use their experiences for learning, not only to improve their own life, but the lives of others as well. This word also makes me think about my grandparents who survived wars in Finland, against incredible odds.

Sisu is a unique Finnish concept, a term that can be roughly translated to mean "strength of will, determination, perseverance, and acting rationally in the face of adversity." *Sisu* is not momentary, it is the ability to sustain your courage in the long term.

My inherited Finnish *sisu* makes me *badass*; I embody it every day by remaining strong within myself and not letting little things get me down. If something bad happens, I no longer stay stuck in the moment; I now consciously learn from it and move forward.

When it comes to me being a *Badass*, one vivid event stands out. A few years ago, I was struggling with four major health concerns simultaneously, which was extremely physically, emotionally, and spiritually challenging. I spent a year in and out of hospital, having all kinds of procedures and surgeries, and talking to so many different doctors that it was difficult to keep track of them all. Every time I met a new doctor, they'd read my medical history binder and say, *"Wow, you are certainly going through a lot."* What a major understatement!

On this particular day, as the newest doctor in my case discussed the best timing for my next surgery, I noticed that he had a Harvard Medical School diploma on his wall. As a former student at Boston University, this brought me an enormous sense of comfort and I felt reassurance that I was in good hands. I listened as he talked about everything I had experienced and, despite having held things together for so long, I broke down and cried as I'd never done before in front of a doctor.

Thankfully, he was very compassionate and explained everything clearly, while showing he understood why I was emotional. When he reassured me that we would find the best dates and times for all the surgeries, and that everything would be ok, something in his voice made me believe him.

After the appointment, having cried all my makeup off, I realised that I had two choices: I could either go back home and feel sorry for myself, or I could pull myself together and go back to work. I went into the bathroom, reapplied my makeup, and went back out into the world—because that's what a *Badass Warrior* does!

My global upbringing gives me a unique perspective because I have been influenced by all the places I've lived. Born in Finland, I grew up in Venezuela, studied at university in Boston and Miami, and now live in Dublin, Ireland. When people ask where I'm from, I joke that I'm Finnish Venezuelan American Irish! But I truly feel like I have bits of all those places inside me, and that they've shaped me as a person.

My international background and the fact that I can speak four languages—English, Spanish, Finnish and Italian—gives me the versatility to reach a lot of people and coach them in different languages.

Even though I am a strong badass, I'm also a sensitive person and, for those of you familiar with astrology, I'm a Pisces Sun with Aquarius Rising and a Cancer Moon. The Pisces and Aquarius parts of me want to change the world and create epic impact. My Moon being in Cancer makes me feel everything very deeply.

Epic Impact is Making a Notable Difference in the World

We live in incredible times where the consciousness of the world is changing, and I believe that I am here to be part of that change. I have always known that my purpose is to help people. Coaching blends three things that have always been important to me: helping people, communicating in different languages, and my spirituality.

Working as a coach is the perfect way to bring these three aspects of my life together. I chose Relationship Coaching because of my own life experiences and the desire to help my clients navigate their relationships with themselves and others.

My coaching journey began fifteen years ago, unexpectedly, through the gift of an Indian head massage while visiting my family in Finland. After having lived and worked in the Americas my whole life, I moved to Ireland with a stop in Finland on the way. Chatting to the masseuse during this incredibly relaxing experience, I learned that she had been trained by an Irish woman who worked as a life coach. After explaining that I was moving to Ireland, she gave me her name and number, so I called her when I arrived in Dublin, only to discover she was preparing to host a weekend retreat in the *Chrysalis Centre* in the town of Wicklow. Although I had never spoken to a life coach, when she told me about the retreat, I felt like I needed to be there, so I immediately signed up to this life-changing experience.

I met amazing, super-talented coaches, made incredible friends, and was introduced to the *Chrysalis Centre*, where I enjoyed many day and weekend workshops over subsequent years. In a full-circle moment, ten years later, I hosted a day workshop in *Chrysalis'* new location in Greystones. After that initial weekend, I decided to become a life coach and the rest, as they say, is history.

It has been an interesting journey with many twists and turns. I cherish all the one-to-one sessions, workshops, talks, and interviews that I have given over the years, and it gives me so much pleasure and joy to see my clients make changes and improve their lives in the process.

Relationships with Self, family, friends, partners, and colleagues, are part of our everyday lives. The better the relationship you have with yourself, the better all the relationships in your life will be.

My course, *Breakthrough to Love*, explores how to improve your relationship with yourself, which will then lead on to improve all the relationships in your life. Everything begins and ends with you.

What is your Narrative?

It's often so much easier to blame someone else for pain, difficulty, or trauma, but one aspect that most people don't think about is that it is crucial to look at your own thoughts, words, actions, and stories. Be aware of the stories you tell yourself and others about your Self, relationships, friends, children, commitment, colleagues, and so on.

When clients come to me, the first thing we work on is figuring out what kinds of stories they tell themselves; when they start to look closely, they will identify their negative and positive narratives. One of the first exercises I give a new client is to write out these stories, preferably on paper, to make it more personal. Time and again, my clients recognise that they tell incredibly negative stories about themselves and any potential partner.

But the good thing is that a story is just a story, and it can be changed even if it has been part of your narrative for twenty years. Once you become aware of your story, you can't "unaware" yourself and, only then, do you have the power to create change. While you can't change anything that has already happened, you CAN change the story that you tell yourself about something or someone.

For example, if you are going through a break-up, you can tell yourself one of two stories. One is that you lost the love of your life and will, therefore, be alone forever. This is negative and potentially shuts out anyone new from coming into your life.

On the other hand, you can frame a much more positive understanding that you are grateful for the relationship and all the moments you shared together. You are thankful that this relationship will prepare you for the next one. This alternate story is full of learning and possibility and opens more doors for you.

When you recognize your negative stories, find a way to turn them around so that they start to work for you and do not stop or block you from future experiences. Remember that the way you talk to yourself is also the way you tell the world to talk to, and treat, you. Be your own best friend and cheerleader, not your own worst enemy.

The Importance of Self-love, Self-acceptance, Self-compassion

People can be so hard and harsh on themselves. Remember to cultivate self-love, self-acceptance, and self-compassion every day, even if it's in small, simple ways. When times are good, it's easy to love and accept ourselves, but it can be hard to do this when we face big challenges.

I love to ask my coaching clients to write a list of a hundred things they love about themselves. Most people think this is a crazy exercise and believe they won't be able to think of one hundred things to love, so I tell them to write as many as they feel comfortable with because the most important thing is to take a moment to cherish and acknowledge their good qualities. If they can't love themselves, how can they expect another person to do it?

In his book *The Path to Love*, Deepak Chopra—who is one of my spiritual gurus—says, "If you want to find the right person in your life, be the right person." For example, if you want to be with a happy and positive person, become a happy and positive person first, because, as *The Law of Attraction* states, "like attracts like."

If you are sad and depressed, there is a low probability that you will meet a happy and positive person because people are attracted to others who are on the same wavelength. You also need to believe and feel that you are worthy of receiving whatever it is that you want to receive, whether it's a relationship or something else.

Our Choices Define Us

Many people define themselves by one single event, or by their jobs, status, or how much money they have. None of these things define you. Remember that you are the one who decides what defines you; unless you give it to them, nobody else has that power.

During my life, I have experienced the highest of highs to the lowest of lows, and everything in between, but there is no single event or circumstances that defines me. I am a combination of all the events and circumstances I have experienced. Be mindful and aware of the words you put after *"I Am…"* as these words define you. And always remember that the only person who decides what goes there is you.

You are so much more than the result of one event in your life, no matter how it has impacted and marked you. I overcame big health challenges, but I'm so much more than that; I am living proof that what doesn't kill you makes you stronger. After I got the all clear, I had to choose what story to tell myself about my experiences. *Would I be the victim, complaining all the time and thinking about how unfair it all was? Or would I use this experience to become stronger and better able to help people?* I chose the latter, which has made all the difference.

My life and health experiences enable me to help and coach people on a much wider scale. I know what it's like to be so broken-hearted that you feel as if you will never recover or find love again. And, most importantly, I know that no matter how bad the heartbreak is, it is possible to recover and find love again. I also understand what it's like to go through incredibly challenging health issues and feel as if you'll never recover but that, with time, perseverance, and strength, you *will* recover, feel the strongest you have ever been, and exceed your wildest dreams and visions!

Awareness is a Treasure

Seeing my clients' "Aha!" moments gives me "cosmic goosebumps," as I call them. The more awareness you have, the more you can change your life and receive abundance in all ways.

For fifteen years, I have envisioned and dreamed of being an international life and relationship coach with clients all over the world. And now, that vision is becoming a reality. During this time, I have learned that if something is aligned to you and your purpose, it will happen in Divine Timing. Everything happens for a reason, even if we don't always understand why, just as people come into our lives for a reason. As the saying goes, "People come into your life for a reason, a season or a lifetime."

We always have the opportunity to learn about our Selves, habits, patterns, beliefs, limitations, and inner strength from our interactions and relationships with others.

Humor and fun are vital to the enjoyment of life. Every day, I laugh and find joy in small, silly moments, and I encourage you to do the same. Remember that whatever you focus on grows, so a focus on positive, fun things will bring more joy into your life. In challenging or difficult times, we must give ourselves permission to laugh and feel joy.

The recent Covid-related lockdowns affected people differently, and we have gone back to the "outside world" with different levels of comfort and fear. If you are scared to go out again, as Susan Jeffers says, "Feel the fear and do it anyway!" Don't let fear stop or block you, acknowledge that it's there and move on. Go forward and always give yourself permission to enjoy life and find joy.

A year after that defining moment in my doctor's office, I was back there to receive the "all clear." To hear that he didn't need to see me again was one of the happiest moments of my life! I cried again, but this time with tears of happiness!

When life challenges you in incredible ways, and you feel that you can't go on, remember that it is our choices in these pivotal moments that define us. We can choose to rise and shine and not be victims of our circumstances because we are *badass warriors* with *sisu* who can get through anything life throws our way!

About Laura

 Laura Rinnankoski is the owner of Laura Rinnankoski International Coaching. She is an international Life & Relationship Coach, NLP Practitioner, Motivational Speaker, Writer, Astrology enthusiast, and a CREA Global Award recipient. Laura coaches in English, Spanish, Finnish, and Italian.

Laura has a very international background: she was born in Finland, grew up in Venezuela, studied in American international schools, attended Boston University, lived and worked in Miami, and presently resides in Dublin, Ireland. Her multi-cultural background enriches her ability to effectively connect and support people from different countries.

She has extensive experience working with advertising agencies and in marketing and sales. She has the work ethic of a Finnish person, the fun-loving personality of a Venezuelan, the determination of an American, and the good luck and humor of the Irish.

Connect with Laura:

2

ABBY SKINNER

BECOMING A QUIET BADASS

When you think about a badass woman, what comes to your mind immediately? A Lawyer? A high-performing executive? A woman who is loud and proud and not afraid to say what's on her mind? More often than not, this tends to be the picture painted.

Society often makes it seem that the "ideal" personality is the extroverted, life-of-the-party, outgoing individual. If you're shy or quiet, you're often viewed as boring or dull, and sometimes even rude. If you don't enjoy small talk, you don't always "fit in" at social functions.

As an introvert, you're often forced to try to conform to what society deems the "ideal" personality.

In elementary school, you're asked to read in front of the class. You have to give presentations in high school. College requires you to take a speech class. For what?

Personally, I've never had any interest in a job that requires me to perform public speaking, so why did I need to learn those skills? To be pushed towards that personality type when it simply isn't who I am? What if it was more important that the "ideal" personality is someone who is genuine? Authentic? True to themselves and loves who they are? That sounds ideal to me.

Growing Up Introverted

As an introvert, I always had a tendency to choose books over people, and art and writing over sports. I had a small group of trusted friends I'd hang out with on the weekends rather than going to loud and crowded parties. However, I also felt I was being pushed by society to fit into societal norms; to be more outgoing, more talkative, more assertive.

I didn't know how. Nor did I want to. It simply wasn't me. So, instead, I became hyper-focused on being really good at the things I was praised for. A straight-A student, never in trouble in class, an excellent writer, the "good" kid at home, the smart kid, not a risk-taker.

I took all those attributes from childhood, all the way through high school, and then into college. Again, striving for straight-A's. Not taking risks, playing it safe.

Destined to be successful because I was "so smart", I actually had no idea what I wanted to do, or who I wanted to be. I was still quiet, loved reading, and found learning fascinating, but society continued to push me to be more outgoing. To get involved on campus, join a club or sorority, and make new college friends.

This was difficult for me. Making new friends was hard. Small talk was not something I enjoyed. I didn't like wild parties; I wasn't much of a drinker, and didn't care about staying up all night long. I preferred spending quality time with a few close friends, and I didn't feel like I fit in.

I changed my major at least three times and eventually graduated college with a degree in Exercise Science, but I had no idea what I wanted to do with it.

Who Am I?

The constant push to be something I wasn't made it hard to figure out who I actually was and wanted to be. I struggled to choose a career path; I wanted to help people, but I wanted it to be in a way that felt good for me. I went back to school immediately and began to pursue a nutrition degree.

After one semester of classes, I changed my mind (again) and decided to apply to Physical Therapy school. I jumped through all the hoops required and was accepted to study PT at the University of Alabama in Birmingham. I was so excited; getting into the school was an incredible accomplishment because over 500 people applied and they only accepted fifty students.

A few semesters in, however, the old feeling crept up on me. I didn't fit. I was never as excited as my classmates about the material, clinical rotations, or getting out to practice. I just wanted to be done with it.

I graduated from PT school and started work at an outpatient clinic, where I saw a variety of patients. For the first six months, I enjoyed it until the familiar feelings began to creep in. I didn't fit. I didn't love this. Days became long, and I went home exhausted, feeling like the proverbial hamster on the wheel. I moved to a new clinic, and then another one, but it was always the same. Only a few months in, the same feelings were back.

Three years into my career, I stopped practicing and took a remote position. At first, I absolutely loved it. I loved our clients and enjoyed the work I was doing on the content side of things. My creative side had been repressed for years; I hadn't drawn or written in so long. All my professional time had been spent working with people and it was so draining that, by the time I got home, I didn't have the energy to do things I loved or was interested in. Now I had the opportunity to be creative as a part of my job, and it was incredible!

This time, it took about eight months for the old feelings to resurface. Once again, I no longer loved my job. I still liked it, mostly, but I didn't love it the same way I had in the beginning. I couldn't help but wonder if I was the issue. I was working from home, coaching entrepreneurs, and getting to write blogs and other pieces of content. What could possibly be missing this time?

A Choice Made For Me

One year into this new career, I lost my job. The company hadn't been growing for some time, so it wasn't a huge surprise and, while I should have been devastated, I wasn't. Honestly, I actually felt relieved. It was the push I needed because, after years of spinning my wheels and chasing careers that I didn't love, I'd finally figured out what the missing piece had been all this time. It was freedom.

Freedom to do what I wanted to do how I wanted to do it, in a way that made sense and felt good to me. I was tired of "working for the man," of being told how to live my life, having success defined for me, and of following the "norm."

I'd been contemplating starting a wellness-based business for a few months, and had put out a few feelers to see if anyone would be interested in working with me to help them improve their own health and wellness. I'm really into fitness; I absolutely love lifting weights and taking care of my body. Fitness has always been an outlet for me and I wanted to help other people learn how to love themselves, create workout routines that work well for them, eat well, and take care of themselves.

Although I'd had a call or two, nobody seemed interested in my offer. I wasn't sure if it was the way I was offering it, if I was charging too much, or maybe it was just because I really had no idea what I was doing. I mean, I'd been a hamster on a wheel for the last ten years; entrepreneurship was brand new to me and, like most people trying new things, I wasn't great at it to start.

After I lost my job, a sense of panic set in. I needed an income. We were very fortunate, in that we could pay our bills and have a little bit left over each month just from my husband's income, but we wouldn't be able to achieve the savings goals we'd set, or pay off a few debts we wanted to knock out. I decided to give myself a bit of time to process my job loss, think about what I really wanted to do, and how I could best help people.

For years, a friend had encouraged me to pursue fitness training, but I'd always been too scared to try. Another friend also encouraged me to do it shortly after finding out I'd lost my job. He was a gym owner and had full faith I'd be successful if I tried. With no job and not many options available to me, I thought, *Why not?* I could try it for a few weeks just to make a little extra cash while I figured out my next step.

Scary Steps

So, I decided to throw it out there and post my offer on my personal social media accounts to see if I could get three or four people interested. This sounds much easier than it actually was; remember, I'm an introvert. Putting yourself out there is scary for most people, but especially for introverts who often struggle with social interaction.

I don't thrive off risk, in fact I usually try to avoid it. At this point though, I didn't have many options and, after a lot of thought, I realized I had to at least try to give myself the option to succeed. If I didn't try, the chance of success was zero.

I usually over-analyze things; I think about them for several days, come up with a plan, and then a backup plan. The more backup plans I have, the more options there are in the event anything goes wrong. This time, I didn't do that. Instead, I decided to keep it simple and posted on social media that I was looking for a couple of people to come and try a free workout session with me. The first one was free, and if they liked it, we could talk about paid sessions.

I thought only three or four people would be great as that would provide a little extra cash to keep us moving forward for a while. Who knows? Maybe it would end up being five or six people and I could do this for a while as I figured out my next steps. Well, I got those three or four people, and then I got three or four more, and then another three or four again.

By the end of the third week of putting it out into the world, I had scheduled over twenty sessions. At the end of the first two weeks, I had four people already committed to continuing sessions, with some of them even committed to at least two days per week!

I was blown away. Not one part of me thought I would have so much interest. I'd even had a few long-distance friends reach out to ask if I could help them virtually! This venture is still very new, and I'm not sure exactly what's going to come of it, but I am sure that it was the first time I'd chosen to pursue something I really wanted, and that aligned with me.

Facing Fear

To make any of this happen, I had to face fear, which is easier said than done, especially for someone who doesn't enjoy the spotlight. Was I afraid of what people would think? That some people would view it as a silly idea, not understand what I was trying to do, or judge me in some other way? Yeah, absolutely.

After having spent so much of my life afraid of what other people thought, I knew that to do something truly different this time, I'd have to overcome that feeling. Honestly, so what if some people think it's silly or don't understand what I'm trying to do? It's my life, not theirs.

For so long, I'd felt pressure to speak up more often, be more social, have more conversations, and just be "more." Now, for once, I wanted to do what I really wanted to do, not what society or other people thought I should do or be. So far, it's working out well because, once we start doing things that are aligned with us and who we are as a person, rather than what others deem we should be, life has a tendency to fall into place.

On this journey, I hope to help women learn not only how to exercise, but how to love their bodies and themselves, and find their own sense of balance in their lives. Taking that first step to put myself out there didn't come naturally, it came from spending a lot of time working on myself. Finding the best alignment with an exercise routine that I loved, learning how to eat in a way that fueled my body well but didn't feel restricted, developing self-care tactics that worked well for me, and discovering how to be me.

A Shift

I'm not sure exactly when it happened, but at some point, a shift occurred. I discovered that society's expectations no longer mattered to me. The shift began when I left the field of Physical Therapy because I knew people would judge me, and that they wouldn't understand it; after all, I'd gone to school for seven years and left the field after only four! I knew they would have something to say, but I was so tired of caring. They weren't the ones living my life or dealing with the emptiness I felt going to work each day.

You see, when society thinks of a badass woman, a successful woman, they usually think of a top performer, an extrovert with an incredible career who is outgoing and speaks her mind. It's true that this woman is badass but being a badass woman is more than just being outgoing or having a successful career. A badass woman is one who is true to herself. She might be a stay-at-home mom who's living her dream of being able to be with her kids each day, or she might be the woman who's brave enough to follow her heart and open her own business, or the woman who volunteers her spare time to help those in need. She could be the woman trying to juggle her career and family life, and take care of herself, all at the same time.

The real badass woman is the woman who chases her dreams in a way that feels aligned with her beliefs. She's authentic. She's real. Not perfect, but trying to do her best in a way that makes sense to her. She's making an epic impact in the world. It might not even be an impact you can see right in this moment, but everything she does impacts someone and what she wants, more than anything, is to do more, help more, and make a greater impact. Always in a way that fits her.

I'm an introvert. I'm shy and quiet, and I don't talk a whole lot when I first meet new people. It used to be something I was ashamed of because, for most of my life, people made me feel that way. I don't feel like this any more because it's okay to be quiet or shy. It's okay to not want to make small talk with every single person in every social setting. It's okay to prefer a little more silence and solitude than the average person. I've never made extroverts feel bad about being loud or overly talkative; I simply accept that's who they are.

I've embraced my quiet side because, although she's quiet, she's fierce and has big goals and crazy dreams she's chasing. She doesn't need to be loud or outgoing to reach them, she simply needs to believe in herself. I finally believe in myself, and I no longer care what society thinks I need to do to be considered a badass woman. I'll continue to be the shy girl who loves peaceful solitude. I've embraced my quiet side and I am going to make an epic impact in this world. Because you can be both quiet AND badass.

And that's exactly what I am.

ABOUT ABBY

Abby Skinner is the Founder and CEO of Happy Living Inspired. A Wellness Coach, writer, and long-term health and wellness enthusiast, she helps women create balanced lifestyles by improving their health and wellness, reducing stress with exercise, improving nutrition habits, and self-care.

Abby has thrived in the health and wellness space for over ten years and understands the importance of a holistic approach for true balance. She knows each person's definition of balance is different and takes a personalized approach with each client. Abby teaches her clients how to have a healthy relationship with food and exercise and prioritize taking care of themselves so that they have the energy and motivation to live out their dream lifestyle. Abby's goal is to teach as many women as possible how to live happy and inspired.

She currently resides in Jacksonville, Alabama with her amazing husband and one fur child.

Connect with Abby:

3

Dr Beth Stuart

Finally, Me

Were you a little puzzled when you first read the title of this book, *Quiet and Badass*? It almost seems like an oxymoron, doesn't it? When I visualize a badass woman, I see a stunningly beautiful, super strong, aggressive type of gal who doesn't take any shit from anybody. Never in my life have I thought of myself that way!

Quiet? Yes, I can be. Badass? Maybe there was another definition than the one above, so I decided to look it up! *Dictionary.com* defines a *Badass* as a person who is "tough, assertive, or independent as to be somewhat intimidating."

Definitely not me, then. I'm really sensitive and always have been. The majority of my life has been lived with passive rather than assertive behavior and, although my core being is independent, for most of my years on earth I have been extremely dependent on others' opinions for my sense of self-worth, love, and well-being.

So, maybe there's a third definition that works for me? One of my friends, and an awesome client, shared with me her definition. Diana said, *"A badass woman is one who is taking charge of her life; making changes for the better; not settling for what others might be expecting of her; living life on her own terms."* Well, alrighty then, I guess I AM a badass!

While it took many, many years to get here, it feels amazing and I'm thankful for the transformation from a socially awkward young woman to the one who now feels comfortable in her own skin.

When you've lived 69 years, it's difficult to remember exactly how you felt at a young age, but I recall being a very sensitive, anxious child, even at the age of four.

Top of the Jungle Gym

My early socialization began with scenes I recall vividly from church K-4 kindergarten. My church besties, twins Marguerite and Caroline, and I were sitting on the very top rungs of the nine-foot jungle gym engaging in four-year-old small talk.

We began to lean over the middle to peer down onto the ground below; to a four-year-old, nine feet feels like a twenty-foot drop. I remember feeling that Marguerite and Caroline seemed braver than me. Maybe it was the way they took one hand off and waved to friends while I sat gripping the bars with clenched hands.

Even at this young age, I recall feeling intimidated by my friends. *What if I said something stupid, and they laughed? What if they thought my shorts were the wrong color or my hair was silly looking?* The twins had beautiful, long, blonde hair. My hair was mousy brown with fringe bangs that my Momma had cut by putting Scotch Tape across my forehead and cutting below the line—you get the picture! My clothes came from *K-Mart* and I felt certain the twins got their clothes from *Belks*.

Four-years-old and I already believed that I wasn't measuring up to my peers. This anxiety in social situations only grew worse from there.

Todd's Disaster

Todd was a handsome young first-grader in my class at Idlewild Elementary. He was very tall with brown hair similar to my father so, of course, being six years old, I fell in love at first sight! Being the shy, quiet girl who only spoke when spoken to, I was sure he had no knowledge of my "romantic feelings." Every now and then though, I caught Todd glancing my way and smiling, which served to set my little heart racing. I remained hopeful until one ill-fated day, when Todd had a very unfortunate disaster and my feelings went from pure love to pure disgust.

Poor Todd had either eaten way too much pizza at lunch or had a dreaded rotavirus. No sooner had my classmates and I settled back into our hard wooden desks than Todd began to projectile vomit all over the floor near his desk in the front row, with my desk only two seats away! The amygdala in my brain sounded alarms that this was a tragic situation.

How embarrassing for Todd. I couldn't imagine being him right now! How was he ever going to get over this terrible humiliation? I very nearly started to cry. To this day, I'm not sure why but this entire scene terrified me. Terry, the cute, blonde-headed, confident girl who sat next to Todd must have known that I was upset because I could feel her eyes glancing in my direction as if to say, *Oh Beth, you poor, sensitive little girl, if only you had my first-grade street smarts and confidence, you would know this isn't the end of the world for Todd. The janitor will clean this mess up and all will be as normal as it was before lunch!*

Get a grip! I could feel Terry saying with her eyes, yet the entire scenario impacted me in a huge way. I went home from school that day and began to worry that I, too, would surely end up vomiting in front of the entire class. Enter school phobia.

Shaking Down the Thermometers

To say that I was a sensitive and socially anxious child is probably an understatement. In the 1960s I'm not sure if "school phobia" was even an accepted term but, today, I know a school psychologist would have diagnosed me with it!

Due to Todd's unfortunate incident of vomiting a massive amount of his stomach contents onto the floor in front of me, every day I was concerned that the same thing would surely happen to me, too. Most days, I ate very little lunch so my tummy was not too full. While all the other kids stuffed themselves with delicious school pizza, I only ate one or two bites and called it quits.

School vegetable soup was also delicious back in the sixties; on one occasion, I remember my friend Nancy slurping down her bowl and the leftover bowls from seven other kids while I watched in shock, thinking, *Oh my gosh Nancy, you'd better slow down. You're going to vomit after lunch just like Todd did!* I was truly worried for her, and myself, as I didn't want to witness a disaster like Todd's again!

So, back to the school phobia. Every week, on three out of the five elementary school days, I slowly made my way up to my teacher's desk and told her that my stomach hurt and I didn't feel good. My teacher usually said, *"Oh, honey, I'm sure you'll feel better soon, just go back to your desk and relax,"* and, reluctantly, I would. But if I got lucky, the teacher sent me to the nurse's office to be checked out. Oh boy, now there was a chance that I might get to go home! The kind nurse felt my head for a fever and stuck the thermometer under my tongue.

Back in those days, all thermometers contained mercury and I discovered that when the nurse left the room to check on another sick child, I could take the thermometer and shake the hell out of it which caused the mercury to look like I had a fever of at least 104! The trick was to put it back under my tongue before Miss Nurse came back into the room. Some days, when I was successful in moving the mercury to just about the right place of 102, voilà!, I got to go home! On one tragic day, the mercury read 107, so the nurse threw the thermometer into the trash can. Oh, the guilt as a ten-year-old was almost too much to bear!

Mrs. Hood's History Class

On a hot Friday afternoon in Spring, at McClintock Junior High School in Charlotte, Ms. Hood, the tall, stern, history teacher, asked me to begin reading the second chapter of our Social Studies book, which was not a problem for me as I was an excellent reader. I began to read but, sometime into the second paragraph, my heart started to speed up. *What's this all about?* I wondered. I kept reading and fairly soon my breathing sped up to the point where, eventually, I couldn't take in a good breath. My voice started shaking and I glanced up at Mrs. Hood as if to say, *Please help me!*

Keep reading! Her stern, dark eyes told me that I'd better not stop; even though she hadn't uttered a word, her glaring eyes said it all. While trying to catch my shallow breath and manage the heightened awareness of all thirty ninth-graders in Mrs. Hood's history class who witnessed my melt-down, I kept glancing up at her in the hope she would give me a reprieve from reading this stupid history book aloud.

What the hell was happening to me? I felt like I was out of my body watching this frightened, voice-shaking young girl lose it in front of her friends. Even worse, one of my "friends" was laughing.

I now know that I had a severe panic attack but, at the time, had no idea why or what I had experienced. That one Friday afternoon affected my life for more than twenty years.

Back in 1967, we didn't talk much about mental health, panic attacks, or anxiety, especially in my family. I had a very loving family, but we didn't acknowledge negative emotions well, if at all. I went home that Friday afternoon and never told my parents or anyone what I had experienced. The shame, humiliation, and embarrassment lived in a place deep inside of me and stayed there for the next twenty years.

Full-blown Phobia

A phobia is defined as "an anxiety disorder defined by a persistent and excessive fear of an object or a situation." I definitely had one!

How did I cope with this subconscious fear of having another panic attack? I changed my life, including doing everything I could to skip school on presentation days. I sat in high school Literature class cringing, wringing my hands, and trying to appear small so the teacher wouldn't call on me to read. Miraculously, she never did! I stopped singing any solos at church. I chose college courses in secretarial science so I didn't have to speak publicly. Once, when I was employed as a day-care teacher, my boss asked me to read something out loud. I shared that I couldn't, or didn't want, to do that and I didn't offer her any explanation. Convinced that something was surely wrong with me, I felt so embarrassed.

These anxiety-producing situations continued until I was around thir-
ty-five-years-old. I vividly remember one of my friends telling a few people, *"Beth
won't say anything unless you ask her a question."*

Sick of this Small Life!

I don't recall the exact day or moment when I knew I no longer wanted to live a
"small" life, afraid of social situations, scared of speaking up in meetings or, God
forbid, speaking in public, but it happened. I wanted to return to college and get
a degree like every other member of my family. I wanted to use my voice to make
a difference in the world. I had this profound sense that there was a whole lot
more to me than I was showing the world, or even had discovered about who I
was!

So, I found a therapist and explained my dilemma. Slowly, but surely, through
intense therapy, reading and re-reading Bourne's *The Anxiety and Phobia
Workbook*, I was able to return to college and finally received my Bachelor's
degree in Sociology from Furman University. Was I completely free from my
fears and anxieties? No, not by any means!

A Work in Progress

Immediately after graduating from Furman University, I took my first professional position as a medical social worker. Although I loved working one-on-one
with the patients, I detested the dreaded Friday afternoon team meetings. Most
of the other twenty hospital social workers freely offered opinions and thoughts

on patients or the topic of the day, but I felt paralyzed in the meetings. I guess it reminded me of sitting in class. It pissed me off when my best friends, Suzanne and June, spoke up so confidently and I knew I could have said the exact same thing, sometimes even better!

Ugh, back to therapy I went! A little more growth. The thing about overcoming a deep-seated fear is that it takes small, incremental steps; in fact, I think I'll always have a hint of anxiety right before a speech, theatre production, or when reading out loud.

Did you read that right? A theatre production?

Getting on Stage!

From the time I saw my first musical, around the age of nine, I was smitten! Could that be me up there one day, acting and singing like Julie Andrews? My entire family was musically oriented. My mother was a music major in college, and she and Daddy would sing together in church. All three of my sisters and I sang in church choirs and music was a big part of our lives. Both my older sisters, Carol and Lee, had participated in school theatre productions and plays but, of course, that was totally out of the question for me until, at age fifty-two, I decided to give it a go.

The local community theatre in Oconee County, SC was conducting auditions for *The Sound Of Music*; what did I have to lose? I knew I was too old to play Maria, but perhaps I would get a small part in the background. I remember reading several sections, singing a song, and going home very satisfied that I had pushed myself out of my comfort zone.

The next day, to my complete surprise, the director offered me the part of Baroness Schraeder, the wealthy, middle-aged woman who hoped to marry

Captain Von Trapp. Wow! My dream was coming true! In the musical, Baroness Schraeder actually sings several solos - yikes! This was more than I wanted but, deep inside, I knew I was up for the challenge. For three months we rehearsed four nights a week, and it was the most intensely tiring time of my life but, oh, so worth it! The sound of the audience clapping wildly as I took my bows was a feeling I'll never forget. Somehow, I came alive as someone else.

Because sitting in a classroom had been such an unpleasant experience, I sometimes wonder why I continued to put myself in that same situation. I suppose, at some deep level, I wanted to fully heal myself, so I headed off to begin a doctoral program at the University of Alabama. Because I lost so many of my young adulthood years staying small and not pushing myself to accomplish things, I decided it just wasn't too late; I had a strong drive to see how far I could go in life.

Sitting in class brought back all the subconscious memories of previous school years. *Should I speak up? What if what I say sounds stupid? These people probably belong here and I don't.* During the weekend intensives, I tried hard to overcome those impostor-feeling experiences, but it was really tough. I seemed to have an extra dose of self-consciousness.

Very early in the program, I'm certain my dissertation chair noticed that my self-confidence needed some help. No sooner had the class settled into a Saturday weekend intensive when my professor announced, *"Beth, for the next three-hour group project, YOU are the President of the University."*

What the f#&k????! This was a nightmare! Shit, I was NOT ready for this.

In the scenario, I had a huge budget, a V.P. assigned to me, and three hours to lose or save money for the university. Timidly, I stood up in front of my university staff and made an attempt to speak; I have no clue or remembrance of what I actually said. The V.P. and staff members got into groups while I made rounds pretending to listen and process the decisions they recommended.

The results at the end of three hours? Epic fail! We lost money and the university went under. Understandably, it was just pretend but, after this activity, I had even less belief that I could lead.

I believed I knew what a good leader looked like, and I sure didn't have it; I wasn't even sure I wanted it!

Finally, Me

Fortunately, the "pretend" university presidency didn't keep me from obtaining my doctorate in higher education leadership. In 2013, my family gathered at the University of Alabama to witness my hooding as Dr. Stuart. It was an amazing day! Because my dissertation topic revolved around fear of failure, procrastination, and college student success, I was offered and accepted a position as Associate Dean of Student Success at Queens University in Charlotte. There were many ups-and-downs in this position and I learned so much about myself and my natural leadership style. I discovered that my unique leadership abilities and talents did not match up well with the management of people.

Through a *Clifton Strengths* assessment I've learned that my top five talents work best when I'm teaching and facilitating groups of people. Since leaving Queens in 2017, I've taught English as a Second Language, and opened up my own business, *emergingYOU,* in 2021. At age sixty-eight, the light-bulb in my head went off and I thought back to all those anxiety-producing experiences I had as a teen and young adult. *Why not take those life experiences and combine them with my knowledge of fear of failure to help others who want to overcome anxiety, and fear of being more visible in their lives?*

We don't need to live small. We're not made to live small. By living small we serve no one. We are created to shine brightly, each in their own unique way.

In quite the departure from my anxiety-riddled younger self, I now confidently empower other women to take back their courage and fulfill their dreams. Taking my painful experiences and combining those with my education, I love to coach other women so that they can transform their lives and live into their full potential.

About Beth

 Dr. Beth Stuart is the CEO of EmergingYOU, a Strengths facilitator, and a Visibility and Camera Confidence Coach. She helps women entrepreneurs discover and lead through their natural strengths, and overcome their fear of being on video so they can shine as their authentic selves and build trust with their audiences.

Having overcome her own fears of being visible, Beth believes that any woman can learn to shine into who she is meant to be, and it's her passion to be a guide along the way. Through her signature program, "Strengths to Shine," Beth supports her clients through small, incremental steps of overcoming the fear that holds them back from success.

Before starting EmergingYOU, Beth held several higher education positions where she supported college student success. She lives in Greenville, SC alongside her three adult children, her loving partner, and her pup, Lucy.

Connect with Beth:

4

CASSANDRA AGUILLON

20/20

The Process

Embracing your uniqueness is a process. You'll uncover pieces of yourself along the way by just living life and experiencing things, as every human does.

Different aspects of your life might be easier to embrace than others, and age can bring a certain degree of confidence as well. It's the luxury that comes with being wisened by more rotations around the sun and relaxing into the knowledge that not everyone's opinion matters.

Sometimes a sizeable chunk of you will reveal itself rather quickly and bring with it many smaller insights, like the Jenga piece that finally topples the tower. Other times it's like removing the smudges from your glasses, with just a section becoming clearer and, still other times, you'll see that you were changing all along and didn't even realize until you stopped to look back.

Deeper acceptance might require intentionality and hard work because it's a long drawn-out process that never really ends; we're too complex for that.

I know it seems obvious but hindsight is always 20/20, right?

The Beginning

I grew up feeling different but, to a certain degree, not caring that I was different. I almost reveled in the fact that I didn't fit in. Weird, I know. A typical Virgo, I was all work and no play, and I loved it. A huge part of me loves to excel at what I do because I take pride in everything. I did well in school and typically got along great with the teachers, although I also recall taking many naps in class.

Oh yes! I was allowed to take naps, even though I'm sure it bugged the heck out of the other kids. Despite working late hours at my first after-school job, I still managed strong grades and always did my work well enough to earn high marks, so my teachers didn't mind when I took a random nap while the other students finished their assignments. I even ranked fourth - in the class ahead of me - and finished high school in three years instead of four. I'll say I earned my naps!

Deep down was a tiny part of me that wanted to be included in the typical high school crowd and their shenanigans, but that was never my path. I hated the idea of being in the spotlight. I'm sure my napping was no fun for them to watch either, but I didn't dwell on it much and, instead, embraced my differences at a young age, not realizing that it afforded me so much freedom and independence.

I was completely free to be me and didn't give a damn what anyone else thought, much to the chagrin of my parents, of course! My poor mother had to claim me as her child even when I spoke up against people.

I once gave a speech at a museum and expressed my thinly veiled opinion during the event about the other kids' disrespectful behavior. Even as a middle schooler, I felt the injustice of not having everyone in our group pull their weight but still claim the credit. When I was asked to speak at the closing, I used my soapbox and said my piece.

My mother's reaction was instantaneous; an epic look of shock and dismay that, nowadays, would be deemed TikTok-worthy!

Thankfully, there were no smartphones around those days or I'd have more of these moments documented. Looking back, I can see why others found me intimidating; I was a budding little badass even as a tween.

Still Waters

As far back as I can remember, my teachers always told my mom that I was an outstanding student, but quiet. They commented that I didn't talk much, as if that somehow negated the fact that I did well in class. As if it was a fault or a character flaw.

Honestly, I hated being described that way. It wasn't relevant to my work, and it's not like I was completely mute or never spoke. I simply didn't feel the need to chit-chat all the time, or get in trouble for talking too much!

Rarely did a teacher understand my sharp wit and dry humor, but one of them once told me the proverb, "still waters run deep," which stuck with me ever since. These words gave me space to be me. I never had to be the loudest in the group to have something of value to say. I don't have to be loud and gregarious to be a badass.

There is so much more strength in standing quietly and firmly holding your ground. I'm not afraid to use my words. In fact, even as a kid, I used my voice to fight on more than one occasion!

I recall arguing with an attendant at the airport check-in when I was about 10-years-old because they'd made a huge mistake and, somehow, separated all the kids in our group onto a different flight than the adults. There I was, just barely taller than the counter, giving them a piece of my mind alongside the parents in the group. I'm a tad more mellow now.

Boundaries

As I moved into high school, I was labeled "anti-social" by someone very close to me, which I found a little offensive. Those were the days when it was still okay to be offended. Ha! It wasn't that I didn't want the company of others, I was just very introverted and fiercely independent.

I'm the type of person who can go into a restaurant to eat alone, or sit in a movie theater by myself. I like simply being without working at entertaining and talking all the time. I can lose myself in a good book and be happy not saying a word all day. I'm lucky to have never felt the compulsion to engage in small talk and am perfectly content with silence.

During my teenage years, I really didn't understand the investment in making connections with people I might never see again. Having said that, while I still keep to myself, I'm glad that even though some things have remained the same, many have changed. People enrich life and I'm grateful to share my life with some pretty exceptional people. I've learned to set boundaries and to be ok with having them.

Part of embracing yourself is to honor yourself and the people you value most. You may find that others only get near and want to chip away at things to cause cracks and sow strife. As someone once taught me, you need to protect what you value and have happy, healthy boundaries. It's basic protection. I don't have to let everyone in, but those I hold dear know they hold a special place in my heart.

There's no need to rely on things or people that are unstable; make sure your foundation is solid so you can build anything you want.

The Big Change

As I headed into my freshman year of university, I experienced the most pivotal period of my formative years when my parents went through an ugly split and ended a more-than-twenty year marriage.

My mom was my rock and anchor growing up; she's one of the strongest people I know and essentially raised me and my brothers as best she could under the circumstances. She was even involved with my friendship circle, and the only mom who was given a nickname, "Cass-Mom." Yeah, we kept it simple! Ha!

She supported me in whatever I was doing at school and was always there at our many extracurricular events. She drove us around and gave her time and energy to raising my brothers and me, as well as our extended family. She's a huge giver and her strength gave me a place to anchor myself in the knowledge that I wasn't too far from the harbor of home and safety.

One particular night, relatively early in their split, is forever etched in my memory. My dad had already left our home, but they still communicated, I suppose. I walked into the house to find mom sitting on the floor of the hallway outside her bedroom. What I saw changed everything; her face was swollen and I have no idea how long she'd been there sobbing, huge body-shaking sobs. She was broken and fragile, two things I had never, ever associated with my mother.

Seeing her in so much pain, and in pieces on the floor, tore me up and made me so freaking angry. I know she was the one with a marriage ending, but I felt powerless to fix things for her, and I couldn't do anything but get mad. I was mad at my dad for leaving, but I was also deeply enraged that he had hurt her. She gave and gave and yet; she was the one that got hurt.

I used my voice and sharp tongue against my dad and it became a charged, vexatious time that was prolonged over several years. My independent streak sure didn't help much here, either. My dad isn't the type to take the bait and return anger with anger. He's not hot-headed in the least, but the divide between us grew for quite a while before any healing started.

I'm grateful it's much different now, but the impact of this big shift is still felt today, as any divorced family knows.

It took a very long time to get to a place where my memories are still sad and there's a sense of loss of what could have been, but my anger is gone and I love my dad. Now, I can see them both as complex humans who had their own paths to forge and navigate.

This experience, and the years that followed, sprouted a need to rely on things I could trust and really count on and, to a certain extent, control.

My love and trust for "data over emotions" grew; I just didn't realize it at the time. Data doesn't have feelings, it doesn't change its mind and cause pain. Even today, I still have a knack for writing things down and making lists to help with decision-making. Writing them down forces me to verbalize and turn the perceived issues into a concrete statement. This helps me see the issues plain as day, simply written, without emotions.

Emotions always make things feel more intense and larger than they seem. They really should come with a safety warning like the side-view mirror on my car. Learning to embrace this, and welcome it as a strength, took time.

Even as I write this, I am making more connections to my past and my present. See, I told you it was a process.

Data-Driven Superpower

2020 upended the world in many ways, but it also brought forth the final barrier I needed to stop making excuses and take control during that time. I was beginning our tenth year of homeschooling, with a third kid in the mix being introduced to some gentle preschool learning.

I had been teaching ESL online for some time and it was that hindsight that hit me again. You see, the kids I was teaching were in China and I could literally see the impacts of Covid-19 taking root from my tiny view through our computer cameras. Some of the students attended classes with me from the hospital or were surrounded by masked family members.

Yet it never dawned on me, or anyone else, just how big things were going to get.

As the pandemic shifted to my side of the world, my local county hospitals made it onto the national news because they were so inundated with patients. I felt a total loss of control, and I'm sure I wasn't the only one.

For a while, I turned to plants, succulents, and cacti that I could focus on and care for, and even put in more hours of teaching, until I just couldn't take it anymore. I hit a wall but still needed to channel all my emotions into something I could do; something I could take charge of.

So, I did what more than 804,000 people did that year; I started my own business. It made so much sense to me at the time. In the midst of chaos, I could channel my superpower of harnessing and interpreting data and facts to start making an impact on the world.

I became a digital marketer, essentially running ads for online businesses and making data-driven decisions every day. It brings so much joy to my little data-junkie heart.

Digital Marketing on the biggest social media platforms is complicated, time-consuming, and perpetually changing, yet, if not handled correctly, it has the potential to make or break a business. These business owners are literally putting marketing dollars into the "ad machine" and expecting it to return even more, so their business will grow and grow.

I've encountered many business owners who love what they do and are so damn good at it too but, when it comes to numbers, formulas, and metrics, their brains shut down. I want them to understand that numbers give them power; the metrics will tell them what's working and what's not. No big emotions tied to anything, just truth.

I want every single one of my clients to feel the power that comes with knowing and owning their data. I don't want any of them to feel powerless.

I deeply know this feeling and it doesn't align with how powerful they truly are and what they're capable of. It's something that my brain understands and, once I learned to embrace this, it became my personal superpower.

I don't have a creative bone in my body, and I can't do what they do; we simply can't master every single part of our business ourselves. It's just not possible, and it's not scalable. You'll always be tied to your business if you go down this path, and there's no living life in that direction.

In the beginning, you may need to roll up your sleeves and do some hard work but, eventually, you will have smart people doing the things that slow you down, so you can focus on the places and activities in your business where you are magical.

Embrace this uniqueness. Channel it and do awesome things. If you fight it, you're only fighting against yourself. I've learned this is my strength and I partner with powerful women who have different strengths, so we both become stronger together.

Embracing

Stepping into my strengths allows me to make a difference. Personally and professionally, I've picked up so much more momentum than I ever had before I realized what my strengths are. Sharing those insights with others and continuing to make a difference creates an impact that will last longer than I will walk this earth.

I want to demonstrate this to my kids by showing them that there's always room to be yourself and that having an equally badass partner at your side makes you limitless. It takes a special kind of strength and self-assuredness to keep up with a strong person, and I get to show my kids all of this.

I'm setting the stage for my children to make their own impact and embrace their own unique strengths.

As a parent, I love this more than anything. It's so incredibly difficult and rewarding to try to guide a young human who is uncannily similar to you, yet completely unlike you in nearly every way! That's parenthood for you.

I know they're getting a head start in life and learning much earlier that they're capable of building their own empire and carving their place in this world. They can take up as much space as they want and be as loud or quiet as they want. I want them to understand that investing in themselves before, and long after, anyone else, is where they will see the greatest ROI (return on investment).

Even being able to show them that the things that are worthwhile are often hard work, and that they'll fail so many times but learn a lesson from each and every time. Knowing that they have someone at their side who strengthens them will only make them stronger.

What is your superpower?

About Cassandra

 Cassandra Aguillon is a digital marketing ninja who specializes in Facebook, Instagram, and TikTok advertising for high-ticket coaches, consultants, and course creators. She also has a highly in-demand service for real estate investors that want to stop chasing leads and wasting time with slow lead-generating methods.

Cassandra has worked with some of the top agencies in the digital marketing space and is now taking back the reins and growing a business that she loves. She has a great deal of passion for coaching and mentoring small business owners and entrepreneurs who need to master their own ads and navigate the ever-changing social media landscape, and cherishes this role in their journey toward success.

Cassandra hails from South Texas where she has been homeschooling her three kids for over ten years alongside her loving husband of eighteen years. She loves traveling with her family and encourages them to have an entrepreneurial mindset.

"Opportunity is missed by most people because it is dressed in overalls and looks like work." — Thomas Edison

Connect with Cassandra:

5

Christina Sims

Grit, Grace, & Gratitude

I wasn't permitted to swear growing up, so admittedly *badass* wasn't a term I ever considered calling myself. Plus, I don't rather care for labels because, in my experience, they often are a catalyst to judgment. But what I've come to learn during this chapter of my life is that we are the authors of our own story. As such, we own the power to give meaning to our words, rather than have them define us. In my eyes, a *badass* is a noun, a verb, and an adjective. Bravery. Audacity. Discipline. In a world that advertises dissatisfaction with oneself, it takes all three of these to have the courage to be yourself. Confidence looks up, insecurity looks around.

I'm not an influencer. I'd rather be a woman of intention and impact. I'm here for the misfits, outcasts, underestimated, and unpopular. The ones who dare to walk the unpaved path as a trailblazer. I see *you*. I'm here to remind you to never allow the validation of others to extinguish your fire. The world has enough copies. Be the template.

If Adversity had a Poster Child, it would be Me

Growing up in a small, rural town where I was typically the only ink spot in a white-papered classroom, I quickly learned there was a particular image for the model of success, and I didn't quite fit the bill. It was hard not seeing many people who looked like me, and even harder feeling like the token black girl asked to explain Black History every February.

I was frequently bullied. I didn't have many friends and was certainly not voted the prom queen, so I hid behind my books. I figured if I couldn't be pretty or popular, I would be smart. My books became my source of solace, my ticket to escape the clique society of high school in which I found myself a misfit, or so I hoped.

Fast forward to my freshman year of college where, in one of my first business classes, a professor told me, *"You are lucky you don't have an ethnic sounding name."* With a puzzled look on my face, I inquired as to why. He explained, *"You should be grateful, because if you did, you would have a difficult time getting hired after graduation. I also would recommend not putting your picture on your resume."*

At that moment, flashbacks of my high school experiences raced through my mind. I could feel the heaviness in my chest, my palms sweating, and the knots in my stomach as I looked around and saw my peers staring at me as I was singled out.

What I failed to realize in that moment was that what I initially perceived as an act of alienation was, in fact, the single greatest piece of advice I received during my collegiate years. He was preparing me for my next chapter of adversity. A chapter of knowledge I would not find in my textbooks.

Unlike many of my peers, I didn't acquire a fancy corporate job right out of college. I graduated during the height of a recession, so at that time jobs were hard to come by unless you had years of experience or happened to have an inside connection. I had neither.

I reasoned to myself in an attempt at humor through the pain, *Well hey, at least it's not because my name sounds ethnic, right?*

However, I was determined to make it. As the first of my family to receive a college degree, I simply *had* to make it. My parents had invested in me and I had to prove I was a return on their investment. I was also the eldest sister, so I put a lot of pressure on myself and felt it was my responsibility to pave that path to success. I could never have anticipated the hurdles that awaited me. After all, during my track athlete days, I was a former sprinter, not a jumper.

My resume fell on deaf ears, so my dad took me to a local staffing agency. My first position right out of graduate school was as an administrative assistant; I felt too embarrassed and ashamed to tell anyone. I was always one of the smartest people in my classes and yet, here I was with my MBA, starting at the complete bottom, making $11 an hour, and still living with my parents.

As a Black woman now in corporate America, I quickly learned I was under a constant microscope. Rather than respected, I was treated as second rate with a specific set of rules that would apply only to me. I was not permitted to wear my hair in traditional ethnic protective hairstyles, as it was deemed unprofessional. As a result, I damaged my hair by constantly trying to straighten it in order to comply with company policies.

I was asked if I was from the inner city or if I was raised by a single mother, only to be met with a look of shock when I stated that I lived in a suburb with both parents, who owned their own home and had successful careers.

I had an amazing boss who understood not only the male-dominated dynamic where we worked, but also saw the difference in treatment I received compared to the other administrative personnel. She made a statement that will remain with me forever, *"Class is knowing you're the smartest in the room without having to say it. Grace is treating people with respect even when undeserved. This may be a difficult start to the first chapter in your book, but sweet girl, know it doesn't end here. Keep going."*

Shortly after, I moved onto another administrative position where I thought I'd have an opportunity to move upward in the company. That hope was soon crushed as I quickly realized I was hired at a place where everyone had practically grown up. Everyone except me.

Once again, I felt like an outsider. I'm sure you've guessed by now that, in this story, I was once again the only person of color. In my first week, I walked into a conversation where I was the topic of discussion and overheard someone remark, *"She must have been hired because of EEO."* By now, my skin was a little thicker and I found solace with two other fellow administrative assistants who quickly befriended me and were well aware of the culture there. They made the days bearable.

Senior management approached me with an important project that would open up the opportunity for a new position within the company. Elated and feeling that this was what I had been waiting for, I spent months creating the systems and a handbook with standard operating procedures that was hundreds of pages long.

Everyone knew this position was being created; the moment I had waited for had finally arrived. There was a big meeting in which the announcement was to be made. I remember sitting next to the secretary, who was my dear friend. She looked at me in excitement because she thought this was finally going to be my opportunity to advance in my career.

But you know when you get that feeling that something is off? That was the feeling I had when I looked around the room. All the faces were familiar, as they were people I had interfaced with while completing the project. All except one.

As I sat there, the head of the department said, *"Thank you Christina for all your hard work on this project. It was appreciated. However, now I will need you to provide us with your handbook as you will be turning this project over to who will be now the incumbent of this brand new position."*

You could have heard a pin drop. I remember looking at my friend, whose face was pale in utter shock. I couldn't breathe. I felt like a brick was sitting on my chest. I couldn't form any words. I silently got up from the table and left the room to return to my office.

Closing my door, I sat at my desk and immediately bawled as my head sunk into my hands. Shortly after, my co-workers entered to comfort me. As they tried to lift my spirits, I couldn't help but question why I wasn't good enough? Why was I good enough to build it, but not enough to lead it, even after being the most qualified in the company?

I had to go. It became emphatically clear that I never would be considered for anything else as long as I was there. I figured as long as I was someone's administrative assistant, I'd never achieve the leadership role I aspired to in graduate school.

Shortly after, I finally landed a position in the field I actually studied in college. It had caught me by surprise because, as a part of the recruitment process, I had to submit a writing sample and the CEO accidentally emailed me about his dislike for my writing, instead of the intended recipient. When I was called for the job a week later, I remember being shocked, as I'd thought I wasn't going to be chosen. What a great reminder to never count myself out!

By this point, I was thinking things would be different. I was no longer an assistant and it was time to show what I could do. However, once again I quickly learned it was a very male-dominated culture in which management heavily criticized, or used my work and presented it as their own with the reasoning being, "I had to earn my way."

One time, I was assigned to present at a conference because a co-worker was expecting his first child during that timeframe. I was elated because I saw it as an opportunity to prove I was ready for a promotion. My boss told me to memorize the original presentation and regurgitate it exactly how they gave it to me. I replied that I could not present work that was not mine and wanted to create my own presentation so I could prove my own merit. I was called difficult; it wouldn't be the first time.

After deliberation by senior management, I was permitted to create my own presentation but with a caveat: I was required to present my original work to senior leadership before I attended the conference to prove it was good enough. Determined, I said to myself, *I'll show them.*

Before I entered the room on conference day, the CEO said, *"Make sure you don't embarrass me."* Then he sat in the front row to watch my every move.

Every presenter received ratings from attendees and I scored the highest. Unknowingly, my presentation caught the interest of a CEO of a global company who was in the audience and contacted the agency to become a client. Specifically, he requested for me to be his Account Manager but I was denied the opportunity. Despite my glowing review and experience, the account was given to the male employee who had been unable to attend. I wasn't even allowed to greet the CEO when he arrived at our office.

By this point in my career, I was mentally exhausted. It felt like a scene from the movie *Groundhog Day* where I continually woke up to the same day; the company names changed but the same scenarios of double standards, disrespect, and hints of discrimination recurred.

That's when the opportunity of a lifetime knocked on my door. I've learned in my life that, when trials are at their hardest, God opens the door to my next adventure.

I received an email from a client I used to freelance for. He was starting a brand new agency and wanted me to spearhead the launch as the Chief Operations Officer. I remember sitting in that Starbucks, trying to hold back my tears of joy, as he presented me with the offer of a lifetime.

All the years of hard work and setbacks felt like they were finally worth it. I attained an executive level position, and I did it before the age of thirty. It felt so good to tell my boss not only that I quit, but that I was going to be in the exact role he worked in. Within three years, I helped turn that agency into a seven-figure business and had reached a pinnacle in my career.

And then, in an instant, my entire world changed forever when my husband and I discovered I was expecting our first child. The thought of motherhood was the biggest shock to my system. My husband and I both were passionate about our goals, so until then, it had been easy to juggle them because it was just the two of us.

Nine months later, I went in for a routine stress test because the baby was late (*took after his mama, of course*) only to be told they couldn't find his heartbeat. In an instant, my heart sank and I was immediately rushed by ambulance to the hospital. All I could think about was how I was going to tell my husband we had lost our son. During the twenty hours of labor, his heart flatlined, twice. After the second time, I was immediately rushed into the operating room to be put under for an emergency Cesarean section without my husband or any clue if either of us would come out of all this alive. I have no recollection of his birth. All I remember is waking up from the anesthesia and asking my husband, *"Did he make it?"*

By the grace of God, my son survived.

When I laid my eyes on my beautiful son, *everything* changed, including my priorities. Then, two weeks later, I found myself facing the greatest adversity of my life; I was told I had to return to work. I wanted time with my son but I also knew that, financially, I needed to provide for him.

I returned to full-time work exactly one month after I gave birth. I still had stitches from my emergency Cesarean section and remember just being in tears as my mother got to nurture and hold my son in those first precious moments, while I had to focus on work.

The three months of bonding I had anticipated while learning about my new world of motherhood were ripped from me. I felt powerless. I felt cheated. I felt robbed. Physically and emotionally, I felt bankrupt as I learned to navigate pumping around the clock while working full time and trying to balance being a present mother and wife.

I came to the realization that there was no balance. My old world and my new world were not compatible and something had to give.

This awakened something in me. I realized that, rather than being in the driver's seat of my life, my life was driving me. I thought back to what my first boss told me; my story was being written, but I wasn't the one writing.

Despite the setback, this time around, I knew what I was capable of. I was no longer going to allow my autobiography to be written by anyone but me. This time, I was taking my pen back for good.

In the middle of a global pandemic, I started my business and called it *Mom Meets Life* as a declaration of me writing my new story. Was I afraid? Absolutely! Here I was with the audacity to launch a business when everything was shutting down. As I looked at my son, I said to myself, *failure isn't an option and I'll be damned if I lose any more time.*

While the world stood still, I kept moving and, to my surprise, discovered many other women were tired of being discredited, discounted, and dismissed. Just like me, they also had the desire to take back their power, command their value, and stand firm in their truth.

Through my pain, I found my purpose. Now I have the true honor and privilege of helping others discover theirs.

I would be remiss if I didn't say that I'm one of the blessed ones. Despite my hardships, I've always had the comfort of a loving family and, for that, I am eternally grateful. I know many of you walk your journey alone. I see you. I see your strength and admire your courage.

There's a saying that goes, "There are no shortcuts to success." In my story, the road to true autonomy passes through adversity first. It may be bumpy, you might even take a few wrong exits, but as long as you keep driving, you'll get there.

The late Jane Marczewski, famously known as *Nightbirde*, once said, "You can't wait until life isn't hard anymore before you decide to be happy."

We get one opportunity to live and that time is short. A dear family friend once asked me what I was grateful for. That's when it hit me. I could list in a minute everything I felt was wrong with my life. It was as easy as breathing. Here I was with so much in my life to be grateful for, so much to live for. Yet, when asked to name the positives in my life, I had to think. It's so easy to become consumed and caught up in the negativity that you forget to celebrate how far you've come and all that you've overcome. That conversation changed my mindset that day, but was forever cemented in my heart when I learned he unexpectedly passed from Covid just a few short weeks later.

You have a message within you that is worth telling. A story burning within you that deserves to be told.

A story left untold is no story at all. I believe that by denying the world of your voice, you do a disservice to the world. The mess in your story is the message someone else is seeking to hear. And you know what? You just might be the one who inspires someone else not to give up and to take that leap.

Your story might be the beacon of hope that lights the spirit of someone in their darkest hour. You just might make an impact. You may be the one who makes a difference. Have the bravery to tell it, the audacity to own it, and the discipline to never give up.

Now *that* is badass.

About Christina

Christina Sims is a mother, wife, mompreneur, and storyteller. She is also a Personal Branding Coach, Marketing Strategist, Copywriter, speaker, and the founder of Mom Meets Life.

For more than a decade, she has led corporate marketing, advertising, and brand development initiatives for global companies. An unexpected near-death birth experience in 2019 inspired her to launch her business where she specializes in helping online coaches and service providers build authority and visibility to become in-demand and premium paid experts.

Christina's mission is to empower women to audaciously own their stories and create profitable businesses by being exactly who they are. Her trailblazing and unapologetic strategies set her apart in an industry focused on perfectionism, trends, and scripted approaches.

A graduate of Seton Hill University, Christina has been recognized as one of Pittsburgh's *People on the Move* and featured in Authority, Thrive Global, Brainz, Self-Mastery, and Pretty Women Hustle Magazines.

Christina spends her time in Pennsylvania, with her husband Justin and their son Greyson.

Connect with Christina:

6

CHRISTINE FREY

I ALMOST DIED TWICE

I almost died twice. I understand trauma, heartache, and loss. I understand not feeling safe, loved, valued, wanted, and cared for. For most of my life, I have felt isolated, terrified, always on guard, and very safety conscious. My father was an abusive alcoholic who made our family fearful and unsafe. My parents fought terribly; they were two broken people in a violent relationship, and my mother had never known freedom. I watched her lose her passion, autonomy, playfulness, and sense of self as we grew up. I did not realize I would grow up and also raise my children with this same destructive pattern.

So many dysfunctional and damaging thoughts and patterns were learned while I heard and saw domestic violence all around me. My mother would try to stifle her cries and screams, yet we knew what was happening. When I was in sixth grade, my mother and I were in a car accident that totaled our car. We stood in an overgrown field near the accident scene as she spoke to the police, scared and crying, her shoulder dislocated, unable to find the car keys that had our house key attached.

The police drove us home and my crying mother went to the back door to try to get into the house. The door was locked, so my mother got a ladder and, using one arm, helped me climb up and get into the house through a window. Once we got into the house, her crying became uncontrollable as she said she had to start dinner so my father wouldn't get angrier.

Next thing I knew, my mother looked at the door as my father stormed in and told her how stupid she was to total the car. Before she could do or say anything, he punched her square in the face, breaking her nose. She didn't have time to cry out before he grabbed her hair and dragged her upstairs while she tried desperately to support her injured arm. He continued to yell at her and, with blood all over her beautiful face, she begged him to stop because I was watching. I backed myself into a corner to make myself as small and invisible as I could. The thing that stuck with me the most was that she never got her shoulder fixed.

There were many good times growing up, but domestic violence was a factor more often than not. When a dysfunctional family is living in this damaging lifestyle, oftentimes the children are susceptible to negative outside influences. From the ages of four to eight, two male "cousins"—who were actually family friends—sexually abused me. While I was in elementary school, no one at home seemed to notice that I was wetting my pants almost daily. I remember feeling shame, embarrassment, and horror as I tried to hide my wet clothes and get to the nurse as quickly as I could for new clothes.

In third grade, the nurse asked me to come to her office and, when I got there, my mother, the principal, a police officer, and the nurse were waiting for me. We never visited that family friend and her two sons again. I learned to play small, feel ashamed of my body, stay quiet, be a good girl, and to keep dirty secrets.

While I was growing up, I had the privilege of attending a prestigious private school, but I felt lonelier than ever. I felt as if I was the only child living in a violent and chaotic home, never shared what I was going through, and rarely had friends over because I didn't want my family secret to get out. It was exhausting to put on a fake smile every day so I could be "normal" like everyone else. The domestic violence got worse during this timeframe because my father was exhausted from working, stressed about money and, consequently, his alcoholism accelerated. There were many times that my mother parked as far away as possible when she picked me up from school, so no one would see her crying and hurt.

It pained me to watch her lose her autonomy, self-love, and identity as she became increasingly fearful and neurotic. She felt trapped because she had no family and kept her toxic secrets from her few friends. She wanted to work outside the house, and tried to do so for a short while, however she was not allowed as she needed to be home for us, to make sure the house was clean, the kids were quiet, and dinner was ready for my father when he got home. He abused her financially, physically, emotionally, and mentally, which was extremely hard to watch firsthand.

I graduated from high school when I was sixteen years old. I had earned money cutting lawns, babysitting, and delivering newspapers and, when I graduated, I got a full-time job which required me to walk a little over two miles each way to and from work. I tried to stay out of the house as much as I could, amusing myself with my friends, and I got a boyfriend.

One night when I was seventeen, I sat with him in the driveway without realizing it was ten minutes past my curfew until I walked in the front door. My father punched me in the face, grabbed me by my long hair and, while screaming at me, dragged me up the stairs to my bedroom. My mother repeatedly begged him to stop, saying, *"Stop! You're going to kill her!"* Then I heard her tell me, *"Be quiet and it will be over soon."*

Never again.

When they went to bed, I grabbed a few of my personal belongings, climbed out my second-storey bedroom window, shimmied down a rain gutter, and ran to a local convenience store to call my boyfriend.

I continued to live fearfully and destructively in a domestically violent relationship that evolved into marriage. When you have a distorted sense of self, safety, and what a healthy relationship should be, you feel comfortable in this dysfunction because it's all you know. Abusers are really good at courting, apologizing, and promising it will never happen again. During our twelve-year marriage, he was arrested for domestic violence, I forgave him, we had two beautiful children, and the violence continued.

The last straw came when he was drunk, yelling and throwing stuff around the house, and nearly hit one of my sons. I had him arrested for domestic violence again, and subsequently divorced him. We were two broken people in a violent relationship, just like my parents.

Continuing my pattern of choosing violent alcoholics, I then married a man with four children. My loyalty to the codependency and scarcity-conscious-ness mindset overruled my common sense, and I failed to get my children, and myself, out of another damaging relationship. I repeated the destructive family patterns and raised my precious children in yet another domestic violence situation.

My new husband was very controlling and was furious when I started college. He stole my textbooks, flattened my tires so I would be late for school, punched out all the light bulbs in the house so I had to study in the dark, and often would not come home in time to watch the kids, so I had to scramble to get a babysitter or take them with me. He was arrested twice for domestic violence.

The second time he was arrested, I left my house and drove to a local convenience store to call the police. My friend, who was also a police officer, came to help me and take my statement. He looked at my swollen eye and disheveled hair, and held me gently by my shoulders as I saw tears run down his face. He said, *"Chrissy, when is this going to stop?"*

I drove myself to the hospital and the police officer came to talk to me. He told me that, when he went to my house to arrest my husband, he was so drunk that he had to be woken up. My husband had wet himself and had no memory of the incident. He started crying, saying he was so sorry, and that I did not deserve it because he loved me and I was a good wife and mother. He asked the police officer to bring him to the hospital to see me before he went to jail, but they refused and, instead, he went straight to jail, as he should have.

Once he was released, he moved in with a friend for a few months because he could not come home while there was a protective order in place. He started anger management classes, therapy, and AA. Meanwhile, I went to counseling, Al-Anon meetings, and domestic violence survivor classes. We started speaking again, and I dropped the protective order so we could become a family again.

I almost died twice by strangulation, once in each marriage. Having two near-death experiences was still not enough for me to leave my second husband. By this point, I had Complex PTSD, and I was surviving, not thriving, in a dysfunctional and distorted sense of reality. I admit culpability for my grievous mistakes, poor choices, and unhealthy decisions as I copied my parents' relationship and raised my children for most of their lives in this damaging environment.

My parents died in a house fire on my birthday, in 2014. I am very grateful that we developed a loving, close relationship where we accepted accountability and forgiveness before they died. Three months later, my husband was diagnosed with Stage Four larynx cancer due to lifelong alcoholism and drug abuse.

He was the best husband in those last three years, when he realized what was important and that his time was short. However, he chose to continue to drink excessively and died from his addiction, not the cancer. Twenty years with him and I held his hand as he died from end stage liver disease at fifty-six years old—the effect of lifelong drug abuse and alcoholism.

My late husband had a longtime childhood friend named Tim, who was my friend as well. Three days before my husband went into hospice to receive a pain medicine pump, he looked me in the eye and said, *"I want you to marry a nice guy like Tim. No more idiots."* I told him we didn't need to talk about that because he wasn't going to die anytime soon. The only reason we were even in the hospice was so he could die peacefully at home, as he wished. He was supposed to come home three days later, but he never did.

I spent sixteen days by his side in that hospice, watching the man I loved die. I wanted to love him enough to save him from his addictions, and death, however I didn't offer myself the same compassion, kindness, and support.

After he died, it took a while for me to grasp that I was free. Living in a domestic violent relationship is challenging for so many reasons because there are many good, happy times as well as terrible times. When I got home after he passed, I was caught off guard as to who I was now, wondering how I could live in a healthy, quiet, peaceful way without fear?

It took forty-nine years of domestic violence for me to finally get out of my own way and seek professional help. I am grateful that I had, and still have, amazing therapists, as I've done a lot of therapy and healing modalities.

Accepting responsibility for my actions, my unhealthy roles in all of my relationships, and forgiveness for myself and others has been cathartic. Leaning into my faith, emotionally mature people, good friends, and my healing work has brought me back to a life where I am thriving. Truly, I am a chain breaker, and I am going to spend the rest of my life helping people who are suffering and broken from all kinds of experiences, especially domestic violence.

I promptly became a Confidential Victim Advocate (CVA) for *A Woman's Place* in Pennsylvania, and I have heavily volunteered many hours for *Tessa*, a domestic violence organization in Colorado Springs, Colorado, where I now live. *A Woman's Place* was a huge part of my safety net and support, so I immersed myself in all aspects of their work to pay it forward and support others.

My mother never knew freedom from domestic violence, but I refused to stay small and stand in shame and guilt. I stand up to create an awareness of domestic violence and the multi-generational impact it has on so many people. Standing up and giving survivors a voice, and listening to them with empathy, respect, and integrity is invaluable.

It is my passion to do this work for myself, my children, family, friends, and everyone who feels alone. Taking the stigma away from this socially pervasive topic helps to cultivate awareness, strip away shame, fear and guilt, and will save lives. Giving people a second chance, like I've been blessed with, is truly an honor and privilege.

After my husband died, I had no intention of getting married right away, as I was free for the first time in my life. My children were grown and I wanted to live! Tim often checked up on me and, on one occasion, came to get me out of my house, take me to lunch, and go on a hike. We started to talk more often and do things together and eventually realized we were falling in love.

Tim and I are now happily married, and it's our first sober relationship. There is no drinking, drug use, arguing, violence, shaming, stealing, lying, or domestic violence of any type. I was used to men stealing my kids' piggy banks, my jewelry, and possessions, emptying our bank accounts, and getting title loans for our cars to fuel their addictions. For the first time in my life, I am with a kind, sweet, gentle, supportive man who is my best friend and confidante.

I am grateful for the time Tim has given me to heal, become a Shaman, and start a business in our home. I don't have to create a safety plan, hide my keys and phone, and I now know men can be thoughtful, honest, and trustworthy. We take care of ourselves as individuals so we are healthier together; we know life does not have to be hard all the time, and we don't have to earn love and respect.

Today, I run my own business, *Centerpoint Healing Services Inc.*, and I work with survivors of domestic violence, sexual assault, addiction, and recovery. Forgiving myself for all the times I saw the red flags as a challenge rather than warning signs was extremely difficult. I will never be the same, nor do I want to be, as I love the person I have become and my soul lessons are truly invaluable. I am very proud to be the owner of a private studio that is an open and welcoming space for all humans.

As a Shaman and Reiki Master Teacher and Practitioner, I offer Reiki to enhance my clients' lives and create transformational awareness. Teaching trauma-informed yoga is offered as well, to help survivors learn how to recognize and tolerate physical sensations in the body.

My offerings teach survivors how to begin deeply healing what needs to be acknowledged, felt, healed, thanked, and released, so they can physically, emotionally, mentally, and spiritually move forward in their lives. The premise of my business centers around teaching them that they are capable of reclaiming their personal power and evolving into the best version of themselves, and to create a safe space where survivors can be heard and respected.

This work is invaluable to me because the ripple effects of kindness and healing are immeasurable. Thank you!

ABOUT CHRISTINE

Christine Frey is a Shaman, Reiki Master, trauma-informed Yoga instructor, and the Owner of Centerpoint Healing Service Inc. She helps people on their journey of healing so they can discover the joy, hope, and blessings they are so worthy of.

Christine combines 32 years of teaching experience in the areas of exercise, yoga, and body movement, which when interlaced with her Reiki practice, and as a Shamanic Reiki Master Teacher, allow her to connect with her clients and provide a safe space for growth and energy. She believes that, as in all life, a healing journey is a continuous path of learning and discovery.

Christine currently resides in beautiful Colorado Springs, Colorado with her husband, son, three cats, and one dog. She also has an adult son living in Pennsylvania.

Connect with Christine:

7

Donna Renee Moody

Stepping Back From The Edge

I never considered myself to be a *Badass*. Always of the opinion that *badass* referred to someone tough, loud, and in-your-face, I knew that definitely was not me; I was always the quiet, terrified one in the back of the room. My definition, however, has changed considerably over the last few years. Now, when I hear the term *badass*, I immediately think of resilience, strength in the face of adversity, and the power to overcome. My definition changed because I changed. I spent the majority of my life being afraid of everything: of being seen; of being heard; of speaking my truth. It wasn't just the fear that held me back, but a deeply rooted belief that I was insignificant and unworthy of success.

Not anymore. I've learned how to overcome adversity, challenge the status quo, and to say what I feel, external approval be damned. I've learned how to embrace my inner Badass. I am the only me there will ever be. No one else will think my thoughts or hold my opinions or express my desires. My "me-ness" is my uniqueness and I can unapologetically say I am extremely proud of that fact because of what it took to discover it.

Just a few years ago, I never would have imagined contributing a chapter to a book. *What did I have to offer? Why would anyone care what I have to say? Sure, I was quiet, but a Badass?* Definitely not.

There's a great quote by Wayne Dyer that I've learned to live by, "When you change the way you look at things, the things you look at change." I've learned to change the way I look at myself and, consequently, I've changed. Now I define myself as determined, empowered, and ready to help, serve and use my *Badassery* to inspire other women to embrace their own epic gifts.

In January 2017, I had been working as a bookkeeper for a small company for eighteen years. The job paid the bills and had a lot of flexibility, which was great, but it no longer felt right. To put it plainly, it was soul-sucking, which is probably why, when the alarm clock went off at 4:00am, I turned it off, sat on the edge of the bed and started to cry. The morning was chilly, but my tears felt warm as they splashed onto my thighs. Life felt like a giant black hole of despair, like I was standing on the edge of a cliff contemplating whether or not to jump. I didn't know what I was going to do. All I knew was I could not go on living like this.

For several months, I'd been feeling physically, mentally, and emotionally drained. I was dragging myself through the days with no energy and even less enthusiasm. I was getting closer and closer to the edge but then, with Divine timing, the Universe stepped in to help.

One day I was scrolling aimlessly through Facebook when a video from an emotional intelligence coach in Perth, Australia, caught my attention. She was beautiful and charismatic, and I instantly felt an energetic connection to her. It was almost as if she spoke directly to me as she offered a free coaching program to the person who engaged with, and shared her posts the most. I commented on and shared every post I could find; I really didn't expect to win, but I did! When I started her program things began to shift almost immediately because her coaching style really resonated with me, so I simply dug in and did the work. Eight weeks later, I was a different person mentally, physically and, more importantly, emotionally. She taught me how to regulate my emotions, tap into my inner strengths and abilities, and claim my power. I realized the reason I'd been so challenged in life was because I was out of alignment with my purpose. This realization changed the course of my life.

For years, I'd had a strong interest in health and wellness. My niece Lisa, a nurse, was doing network marketing for a health and wellness company and introduced me to some of their products. All of them were clean, high quality, and gave me lots of energy. With my newfound energy and empowered mindset driving me forward, I decided to enroll in nutrition school. I started to research schools online and came across one offering a health coach training program. Lightbulb moment! *Health, wellness, and coaching all rolled into one? What could be better?* I could pursue my passion for health and wellness and help women at the same time. This was the pivotal moment for me; I wanted to take the gift of coaching I'd been given and somehow pay it forward, and now I had the perfect opportunity.

Here is the point where I need to add a little context: I had never before in my life had a desire to help people. I didn't see myself as the helping type. Being introverted made me want to avoid people, not go out of my way to help them. Not to mention that I also had a pretty screwed up idea of what "helping" looked like. I had visions of volunteering at a soup kitchen or cleaning up litter. No, thank you. Not my scene. I'm aware of how totally selfish and screwed up that sounds, but it's the truth. Well, it was the truth before I did the work on myself. Doing the inner work taught me how to get outside of myself, to see the bigger picture, and how we're all connected. By helping others, I help myself. Life is circular, and everything comes back around.

In September 2018, one month before my fifty-sixth birthday, I enrolled in the health coach training program. I loved everything about it. The training was fascinating; I learned so much about nutrition, but also about how important the other aspects of our lives are to our health and wellbeing. Our careers, relationships, finances, environment, and so many other facets impact how healthy or unhealthy we are. Like a sponge, I soaked up all the knowledge they could pour on me. It was heavenly.

Not everyone was happy about my desire to change the course of my life at the age of fifty-six. There were plenty of unsupportive wet blankets trying to discourage me. Ironically, the more vocal they became with their discouragement, the more determined I became. I graduated from the health coach training program in September 2019 and immediately dove into more classes. I studied life coaching, Neuro-Linguistic Programming, advanced nutrition courses, Reiki, and other holistic modalities. I was hellbent on having as many tools in my toolbox as possible in order to help other women live their best lives.

I'm not going to lie, as much as I loved what I was doing, there were moments when I wanted to quit. Study time had to be crammed in between a full-time job and family responsibilities, which meant lots of late nights followed by very early mornings. I was chronically sleep deprived, which led to hormonal imbalances, which led to unrelenting stress, which led to weight gain. Becoming an unhealthy holistic health coach wasn't exactly a great confidence booster, and it's an issue I'm still dealing with, but I know how to correct it. It's a slow process, but I'm getting there.

More important than all the incredible techniques I've learned is the person I've become in the process. I've become confident in myself and my abilities, learned to trust my intuition, and regulate my emotions so they no longer rule my life. I've also developed a spiritual practice that allows me to decompress and connect to my higher self. My being has leveled up and through the process, and I've been gifted with the ability to serve.

Coaching women through health and life challenges has been the greatest privilege. So many women feel stuck, like they are prisoners in their own lives. Many are unhealthy because they've put the needs of others before their own. Some just feel lost and directionless because they've never taken the time to ask themselves what they really want in life. Working with these women has helped them find answers to the questions they've been asking themselves, but haven't been able to answer on their own. I am honored to help women discover that the answers they seek are within themselves. Every coaching session I conduct leaves me feeling exhilarated. Watching women discover the answers they've buried within themselves is the best feeling there is. I love seeing their faces light up when they reach that "aha" moment, when they realize how capable, resourceful, and powerful they truly are. All women deserve to discover this power within themselves. This is the power of coaching.

It has become my mission to help as many women as possible discover their power and take control of their lives. Empowered women have the ability to change the world. An empowered woman is a better mother, partner, daughter, and sister because she is secure in her being. She knows she can handle whatever life hands her because she has the strength and the tools to do so. An empowered woman is a force to be reckoned with.

Becoming a holistic health coach is the best decision I ever made. It has allowed me to meet amazing women who have helped me as much as I've helped them, and who have allowed me to grow as they grow. The coach-client relationship is reciprocal, a two-way street. Still, I believe I receive more than I give most of the time. My clients are the jewels that put sparkle in my life. Every single one of them is unique and incredibly special. My clients are the Universe's way of letting me know I am finally aligned with my purpose; they changed everything for me, like cleaning a dirty window to finally allow the light to shine in. The cavernous darkness waiting at the edge has faded and I've been able to step back and return to the light. Living in the light is like being reborn and seeing the world for the very first time. Everything is new because I see it with new eyes. I understand why I had to go through the darkness; like the seed that germinates in the dark earth or the caterpillar in its dark cocoon, metamorphosis happens in the dark and what emerges into the light is something completely different. I am different.

Of course, every day isn't sunshine and rainbows. Life doesn't work that way. There are good times and bad times. The difference is in how I handle the bad times. Treating myself with kindness and grace serves me better than beating myself up. I still have to get up at 4:00am, but I no longer sit on the edge of the bed and cry. I still go to the bookkeeping job, but I know it is not my life. I get to coach clients in the evenings and I look forward to those sessions all day. I'm playing the long game. Divine timing will let me know when to let the bookkeeper go and completely embrace the coach.

In the meantime, I continue to learn, grow, and be better today than I was yesterday. I'm able to enjoy the process, knowing everything is unfolding exactly as it should, according to Divine timing; no more trying to force the flower to bloom. Letting go of the need to control, and knowing I'm always right where I belong, is so liberating and stress relieving. The road to the edge was dark and treacherous. There were rocks to trip over and holes to fall into. I felt lost, powerless, and constantly afraid while I traveled. Stepping back from the edge allows the light to shine, and navigating away from it becomes easier. I can see the obstacles and pitfalls and either avoid them or plan how to tackle them without all the drama, which makes the journey much smoother.

Life is all about the journey of going from fear to freedom, from confusion to clarity. I'm only now beginning to realize how lucky I am to be able to walk this road. What a gift I've been given to travel the path freely and make my own choices along the way. I get to choose what serves me instead of what holds me back or keeps me stuck, to choose with intention and awareness rather than fear and confusion. Someone once asked me, with rolled eyes, when does this journey end? One day, I'll leave this physical body behind and return to wherever spirit dwells. I guess that will be the end but, until that day, I'll keep on moving forward.

About Donna

Donna Renee Moody is the principal of Donna Renee Moody Holistic Health Coaching. Donna believes it is the birthright of every woman to be healthy, happy, fulfilled, and empowered.

She uses her extensive background in Integrative Nutrition, Neuro Linguistic Programming, Reiki, and other holistic modalities to help women thrive in the 5 Pillars of Health, which are the physical, mental, emotional, social, and spiritual aspects of life.

Donna's mission is to help women heal in body, mind, and soul and to guide them into alignment with their purpose so they can shine their light in the world. She tailors her one-on-one coaching programs to the bio-individual needs of each client in order to serve them at the highest level.

She currently resides in sunny Southern California with her soulmate and best friend, her husband.

Connect with Donna:

8

Jennifer Perri

Paralyzed to Empowered: 56 Days That Transformed My Life

Out of the 18,668 days I've been on this earth, a period of fifty-six days completely changed my life.

I went through so much during the first half of my life: abuse, divorce, loss, and periods of tremendous despair. It has taken well over twenty years to heal from what I've already experienced—but I didn't realize that I was merely "in training" for these fifty-six days.

Almost two decades ago, I decided to take the "mess" of my life and make it my "message." I knew my experiences up until that point would help other women who were facing adversity in their own lives; my story would become their survival guide and a resource as they faced their own struggles.

As a result, I've spent the past twenty years helping women transition through the toughest seasons of their lives. Many have been through divorce or abuse, some have lost their husbands or have battled with health issues. The common thread all these women share is the desire to reclaim power over their lives and finances, so I use my life experiences, education, and expertise to help them pick up the pieces and create the lives they desire. Every single woman has a different, unique story and I've been very blessed to have built a life helping others.

In December 2021, I was enjoying the hustle and bustle of the holidays as I prepared for another wonderful Christmas with my family. I'd had surgery at the beginning of the month, which caused me to slow down a bit but, by the week of Christmas, I was in full swing and loving every minute of it.

Christmas is my favorite time of year, and this year was no different. My husband was locked away in the kitchen creating amazing Italian dishes for Christmas Eve, one of our sons was flying home from studying abroad in South Korea, and we had a wonderful family holiday planned up in the mountains.

I woke up on the morning of December 20th with a laundry list of things to do but didn't feel great. My legs felt very heavy and sort of tingly, but I brushed it off as having slept funny or some other quirky thing. One of the items on my "to-do" list was to see my chiropractor for a routine visit. When I told her what was going on, she thought maybe I had pinched a nerve or some other minor issue. I spent time on the decompression table, which seemed to help, and we booked another appointment for two days later, just to see how I was feeling.

By the time I returned to see her, it was getting worse; I couldn't drive or step up onto the curb without pulling my pant leg to help lift my foot. Although I was getting scared, I tried to play it cool but my husband and chiropractor were not hiding how they felt at all. After a serious conversation, I decided I'd go to the hospital simply as a precaution.

As we lived in the mountains, about an hour outside of Atlanta, I wasn't exactly sure what type of answers we would get at the hospital but, thankfully, they were able to help quickly. Desperate to be home for Christmas, I made sure all the medical staff knew that I was merely there as a precaution and, regardless of what they found, I wouldn't be staying.

After a series of tests, which included an MRI and a spinal tap, we had our answer. They diagnosed me with a very rare neurological disorder called Guillain-Barré Syndrome (GBS), in which the body's immune system mistakenly attacks its peripheral nervous system, the network of nerves located outside the brain and spinal cord. As a result, the nerves cannot transmit signals efficiently and the muscles begin to lose their ability to respond to the brain's commands, which causes weakness and, in some cases, complete paralysis. The weakness comes on extremely fast, but recovery can take months, if not years.

There's no known cure for Guillain-Barré. I'd never heard of it before, but my husband and I were on a mission to learn as much as we could as quickly as possible.

In a significant twist of fate, the female ER doctor had personally experienced this rare syndrome years earlier; within hours of her diagnosis, she was on a ventilator fighting for her life. After a whirlwind of phone calls and discussions with the medical staff, I was informed that they were going to evacuate me by air to whichever state had the infusions I needed to stop the progression of GBS.

Not only was I not going to be home for Christmas, but it also looked like I wasn't even going to be in the same state as my family. It felt like an out-of-body experience.

Through many prayers, and the persistence of my husband, they were able to secure the five-day infusion treatment in Atlanta, so I felt a measure of comfort in knowing I would be within driving distance from my family. As a precaution, they moved me to the Intensive Care Unit for the night in case the spreading paralysis compromised my lungs and stopped my ability to breathe. My husband wasn't permitted to stay, so he went home to regroup as I lay in the ICU attached to machines and monitors, simply trying to process what was going on.

It didn't seem real. I couldn't wrap my head around what was happening. I felt alone, scared, uncertain, and completely helpless. Sleeping was out of the question. As I lay there, I could feel myself losing feeling in my body. I wanted to scream; I wanted to throw things; I wanted to cry; but I couldn't do anything.

The morning came, and it was time to be loaded into an ambulance to make the hour-long journey to Emory Hospital in Atlanta. As I was being transferred to the stretcher, I could barely move my legs and hips, and I had a strange tingly feeling in my back and hands. The paralysis was spreading quickly. I started to feel a tightness in my chest and it was hard to take a deep breath, which scared me more than anything.

A room was waiting for me at the hospital and, within hours, I received the first of five infusions; I felt comfort in knowing that the treatment had begun. But the only thing I could think of was that it was two days before Christmas and, for the first time ever, I wouldn't be home to share the holiday with my family. I was devastated.

Over the next couple of days, my sweet husband and sons proceeded to decorate my room at the hospital with a mini artificial tree and festive lights and decorations. They hugged me and assured me that all that they wanted for Christmas was for me to get better so we could celebrate later. I have the most incredible family in the world.

Christmas came and went and, by the day of my final infusion, I could no longer move my legs. I'd completely lost the ability to walk and could not feel anything from the chest down. If that wasn't enough, the paralysis had moved to the right side of my face, and I couldn't smile or close my eye. I had to wear a patch to sleep so my eye wouldn't dry out. My neurology team discussed putting me back into ICU and prepared me for the possibility of ending up on a ventilator.

I couldn't keep up with what was going on; everything seemed to be moving so fast and decisions were being made for me. I felt completely out of control, which was not who I was and certainly not a reflection of the life I led.

My husband, my rock, assured me at least a hundred times a day that I would get through this, that WE would get through this and that, no matter what, he'd be by my side. In the hospital, he was able to stay with me the whole time and, within a couple of days, became my primary caregiver; he did everything short of giving me my medications. He was there for every scary step of the way and continues to be the driving force in my recovery.

The pain that comes along with GBS is indescribable. I couldn't sleep; I couldn't move; I couldn't get comfortable. As the nerves began to heal, I felt like someone was continuously shocking me from my head to my toes. Speaking of my toes, they felt frostbitten, and I carried an image in my head that if anything or anyone bumped into them, they'd snap off, one by one.

But, after 10 days in the hospital, my team approved my move to rehab. Because of my condition, I needed to be in a rehab that was within minutes of the hospital in case my health deteriorated. The head neurologist stood at the end of my bed and told me that, although he felt optimistic about my recovery, they were projecting about a 90% return to who I was before—and that it would take time. A long time.

Yet, for the first time, I felt somewhat optimistic. There was a glimmer of hope in this current dismal situation.

Another, shorter ambulance ride later, I was admitted into rehab in a room that I'd share with another person with Guillain-Barré. Her name is Gail and she will forever be someone very important to me. A little ahead of me in her recovery, Gail quickly became my motivation and source of encouragement.

Entering rehab was scary; I was terrified that I was going to be stuck there forever. Completely immobile from the waist down, I couldn't feel my arms, hands, or entire torso—front or back—and my face was still partially paralyzed. I was unable to dress or wash myself and had to depend on my husband, the nurses, and the therapists for everything. Bright and early every morning, the nurses would be there to get me ready for the day, and then I'd wait to be picked up to go to therapy.

On my first day of rehab, the reality of my condition hit me like a ton of bricks. I lay there on a hospital bed, completely incapable of moving, wearing a Depend, staring at the ceiling, waiting for someone to come and literally slide me out of bed onto a wheelchair. I remember asking myself, *Why is this happening to me?* Part of me wanted to give up and stop fighting because I couldn't see the road in front of me. I couldn't see the return to the beautiful, busy life I shared with my husband. I felt like a burden. As though I was losing everything.

But I wasn't.

I knew I had a very simple choice to make—stay bitter or get better.

Obviously, I chose the latter.

Every day, I'd pray that I would walk that day. I celebrated the tiniest improvements with my husband, roommate, and therapists. If you'd told me that at fifty-one years old, I'd have to relearn how to write, feed myself, dress myself, and walk, I'd have told you that you were crazy. But there I was, doing all those very things.

Gail and I spent a lot of time talking, crying, laughing, comparing symptoms, and bonding during the hardest time in both of our lives. I got to a point where the question, *Why?* turned to, *What is my purpose in all of this?* I had so many conversations with the people taking care of me. While they were motivating me to stay strong, I was inspiring them to go out and seize the lives that they wanted.

It became clear that I was right where I needed to be at that moment in my life. If it wasn't for GBS, I would have never met the people I did. Maybe they would never have received the encouragement to change their lives because they'd never have had the conversations they needed to have. I learned to find the blessings amid the chaos.

Overjoyed and terrified, I was finally allowed to go home. I'd made huge strides after a couple of weeks in rehab but was still unable to walk. I knew that being home, immersed in the love of my family, was where the true healing would begin.

During my first month at home, I spent A LOT of time thinking, mainly because I couldn't do much of anything else. My husband did everything for me, and I mean everything. The cooking, cleaning, laundry, taking care of our dogs, and taking care of me, all while working a full-time job which, thankfully, he was able to do at home. He encouraged me when I told him I was afraid I'd never walk again. He corrected me, lovingly, when I told him I felt like a burden. He wiped my tears away when I told him how frustrated and scared I felt, and reminded me how strong I was when I was completely emotionally and physically vulnerable.

I'd always been told that being vulnerable was a sign of weakness, but that couldn't be further from the truth. Acts of courage are impossible if you don't first put yourself in a vulnerable position. He allowed me to go through all the stages of healing that I needed to at my own pace. He's an authentic example of "in sickness and in health."

I couldn't walk for fifty-six days. It's truly been the most difficult yet transformational time in my life. As I sit here today, I'd consider myself pretty much "back to normal," at least from the waist up, as I continue to astonish my doctors and those who've followed my journey. I know I still have a way to go as far as making a full recovery, but I'll get there. I've learned many things about myself, the depth of the love of my family and friends, and I've also learned some very important life lessons, too.

Find Blessings in the Chaos. I didn't understand why this had happened to me or what this experience was trying to teach me. There were so many blessings that I almost missed because I was too busy feeling sorry for myself. When life is pulling you in a bunch of different directions and you feel overwhelmed, keep your eyes open for the blessings that are right in front of you.

Embrace Your Tribe. I am blessed to be surrounded by an amazing group of family, friends, and clients. I didn't realize the depth of their love for me and willingness to help until I needed them the most. The phone calls, text messages, words of encouragement, gifts, and flowers were truly overwhelming. I found my tribe and will forever cling to them. Find your tribe. Surround yourself with positive energy only. Never take those who love and support you for granted.

Seek Gratitude in the Grief. I have tried to live my life with an attitude of gratitude, no matter what was happening. That became very difficult for me during this time in my life. We are often grateful for the big things, but don't take the time to be thankful for the small things. The ability to smile, write, walk, or hold someone's hand—be grateful for it all.

Find Opportunities in the Obstacles. When staring in the face of adversity, don't doubt yourself and never, ever give up. We learn so much from the speed bumps that are put in our path in life. Be sure to look for opportunities in the obstacles. There will be people who will take your lead and overcome hurdles in their own lives just because you led the way.

Make Your Tests Your Testimony. In my life, I have faced more tests than I ever thought I would. I thought for sure that some of them were going to beat me. But, each time, I found the strength and courage inside myself to persevere and weather the storm. No matter what you face, and the tests you're given, keep moving forward.

Be the Hero in Your Story. Our life is like a book; it contains many chapters and characters. You will go through many experiences and meet many people. Some of those people will encourage and support you, while others will doubt and belittle you. People come into our lives to bless us or to teach us a lesson. No matter who the characters are in the book of your life, do not let them tell you who to be or allow them to write your story for you. It's your story—be the hero in it.

Never let anyone put conditions on your life. Surround yourself with people who uplift you and see your strength when your vision is cloudy. And only live life on your terms, no one else's.

ABOUT JENNIFER

 Jennifer Perri is an Empowerment & Divorce Coach, Registered Financial Consultant (RFC), and Best-Selling Author with two decades of industry experience. Jennifer educates and empowers women with resources that elevate financial literacy, mindset development, and divorce support to create and cement true independence.

She has been featured in the media as a thought leader, appearing in publications including ABC, NBC, FOX, CBS, Vanity Fair (February 2022, *Atlanta Woman Feature*), The Tycoon Magazine, The Boston Globe, Newsweek, Fortune, and Forbes. In addition to her hands-on work in the field with clients, she was a contributor to the Amazon best-selling book, *Dare to Succeed* with Jack Canfield, creator of the *Chicken Soup for the Soul* series.

Jennifer is the host of two podcasts, "The Smart Money Gal" and "Conversations that Connect Us" and is a sought-after speaker for women's organizations and community groups of all kinds.

Connect with Jennifer:

9

Jenny Alberti

The Quiet Ones

Most people would likely explain that the word *quiet* represents peace, relaxation, and calm. The word *safe* may even come to mind. If you asked them to describe what quiet looks like to them, they may envision themselves sitting lakeside in an Aerodeck chair as the silvery reflection of the moon slowly and gently dances across the top of the glass-like water, the only sound being the crackle of the campfire and chirp of crickets.

For me, the word *quiet* has represented a much different picture. In the past when I heard it, I'd get anxious and my heart would begin to beat faster than its normal seventy-seven beats per minute. I could instantly feel my breathing get rapid, shallow, and restricted. Strange, huh? Well no, not for me.

As an introvert who naturally listens more than I talk, and observes more than I participate, I often have to deal with expectations, questions, and judgments. My whole life I've been told that I'm "too quiet." Whatever the imaginary threshold for quiet is, apparently, I have regularly exceeded it and became conditioned to believe that "quiet" meant "bad" and that something was wrong with me. This message was delivered to me by teachers, friends, coworkers, bosses, job interviews, TV shows, movies, and social media.

I spent many years of my life feeling bad about how I interacted with others. I agonized over what they thought of our conversations, hoping I talked enough for them to think that I was enough. Enough to fit in, get the job, win the promotion, be invited to the party, sit at the table. And the list goes on.

But those times are in the rearview mirror.

I've learned that what society expects, thinks, and feels is none of my concern, nor is it one bit of my problem. I get to be me. I get to be all of me, exactly the way I was meant to be—quiet, quirky, and calculated. And you know what? It feels so good being the **me** I came here to be.

There is a terrible misconception that introverted people lack confidence. While I am sure there are plenty of introverts who also suffer from a lack of confidence, it's not compulsory. It's surely not **my** truth. In fact, embracing my uniqueness and living true to myself provides me with the utmost confidence. By confidence, I don't mean that I'm sure I will always succeed at whatever I do, but that I have the courage to find out whether I succeed or fail. I like to think that the attitude that drives my behaviors makes me a *Badass.*

I strive to be the kind of badass that I have always admired. She's the one who has faced adversity, stood in her truth, pushed onward, and always looked good doing it.

She's Eleanor Roosevelt on December 7th, 1941, addressing "the free and unconquerable people of the United States." She's Rosa Parks on December 1st, 1955, in Montgomery, Alabama, refusing to give up her seat. She's Hillary Clinton on September 5th, 1995, declaring to the United Nations that, *"Human rights are women's rights and women's rights are human rights, once and for all."* She's my mom, Jackie Alberti, on December 16th, 2015, getting behind the wheel of her yellow Camaro, five weeks after respiratory failure and a heart valve replacement.

My hope is to be as badass as these women by remaining true to myself, and I hope to inspire a world of others to do the same. It's been a long road to get to this point of self-acceptance.

Picture it: California, 1987.

Bright colors, denim jackets, and legwarmers were the rage. Bon Jovi's *Living on a Prayer* was #1 on the music charts, *Dirty Dancing* taught us that "Nobody puts Baby in a corner," and President Regan urged Gorbachev to *"Tear down this wall."* For this bright-eyed, tomboy-ish five-year-old girl, it was a great time to enter society via the public education system.

Creative with a big imagination, I spent a lot of time coloring and drawing, and I loved stories. Often I would tell my own vivid stories to my family about tiny make-believe creatures I called "Mogies." Before my dad left for work each day, I made sure to pick up a few Mogies by pinching them between my thumb and index finger and dropping them into his lunch box. These tiny creatures had protective powers and were wonderful companions, both of which I believed my dad needed while away at work.

A persuasive child who loved art and music of all kinds, I somehow convinced my dad to give me one of his record players. He placed it on the top shelf of my white three-row bookcase in my bedroom, along with one "45″ single. The song? A 1961 hit called *"Run around Sue."*

I FREAKING LOVED IT! I'd crank up the volume as high as that little record player would go as I danced and sang in my room, my little feet bouncing up and down on my rose-colored bedroom carpet. *"Hey! Hey! Keep away from a run around Sue!"* I'd sing, happy and content to be jammin' to 1960s rock n' roll by myself in my bedroom. What a cool kid, am I right?

In September of '87, it was time for me to start kindergarten at the elementary school a few blocks from my house. I had gone to Pre-school so was already warmed up to going to school, although I didn't love the idea of being away from home; I'd much rather be roller skating in the driveway or playing ball with my dog, Maggie, while Dad worked in the garage. But, alas, it was time to start my education.

Every day, my teacher gathered us in a circle around her upright piano. She would play as she sang songs to the class and urged us to join in. My favorite was *Old Man Tucker* because the guy in the song washed his face in a frying pan and combed his hair on a wagon wheel. My five-year-old self really got a kick out of the lyrics. But I also remember feeling more comfortable hanging back just a bit from the rest of the kids in the circle. That's if I could get away with it. Often, I was urged by my teacher to move in closer. I wanted to enjoy the songs and stories, but in my own space, like I was able to at home in my room.

One day, my teacher called a conference with my parents to let them know she was recommending I be put in "Early Birds," an extended learning class for students who needed extra help with reading. My mom couldn't believe what she was hearing as my teacher explained her reasoning for the recommendation. She told my parents that I was extremely quiet and she feared that I was falling behind. *"The quiet ones are always the ones who are lost,"* she said. My mom implored her to take another look at my reading and my teacher agreed.

When I read to her one-on-one, she was shocked to find I was reading at a *third*-grade level and proved that my quiet and reserved demeanor didn't mean I couldn't read or that I was falling behind. I taught my teacher a lesson in introversion that day. Needless to say, I was never an "Early Bird." Mrs. Vogel apologized to my mom for years after that, saying, *"I can't believe how wrong I was about Jenny."*

It wasn't Ms. Vogel's fault that she believed *quiet* meant *lost*. This is an example of what is called "The Extrovert Ideal," a term made popular by Susan Cain, one of my favorite authors and fellow Introvert. Our society has idolized the sociable, outgoing, charismatic personality for generations. It's still common for teachers to believe that the ideal student is a talkative, willing participant who loves group activities. That wasn't me. But, as my teacher learned, it didn't mean I couldn't read or that I was lost. What it did mean was that I preferred one-on-one interactions, and that I simply liked my own space and was wildly independent. Kindergarten marked the beginning of my experience and battle with the "Extrovert Ideal."

I strayed far from this carefree and imaginative Jenny. That little independent girl who loved art, writing, singing, and dancing all by herself became anxious and full of confusion. Questions filled and swirled in my head at all times. *Why is it so hard for me to speak up in a group of people? Why would I rather come down with the flu than show up at an event? Why do I feel like I have to perform in order for people to pay attention to me?* And the biggest question, *Why do I constantly have to prove that I belong?*

I became addicted to the approval of others. I craved and sought after feeling accepted.

An Observer and a Thief

At the 2017 *Golden Globes*, Viola Davis presented Meryl Streep with her Lifetime Achievement award. In her introduction, Viola said Meryl was *"like a high-powered scanning machine recording you. She is an observer and a thief."* Those words felt electric and familiar; they reverberated deep within me like the opening riff of my favorite song, *Barracuda*. It was as if Viola Davis was talking about *me*!

At thirty-four years old, I was just beginning to discover the word *Introvert* because it just wasn't something people talked about. Even then, I still didn't truly know what it meant, but I did know that I scanned people all the time. I also knew that I allowed everyone else to do the talking as I studied and took notes to use to my benefit later. No one expects that tuning into an awards show would yield such a profound lifelong impact. But this is what happened to me as I sat on my couch hanging on to every word Viola Davis said.

If Meryl Streep was being celebrated for a lifetime of achievements that she accomplished by being true to herself, and she and I shared some personality traits, then maybe I could find success being me too. After all, up to this point, I was miserable living life as the square peg being forced into a round hole. If only I could be appreciated and seen the way Viola saw Meryl.

Quiet observation of my colleagues and bosses helped me revolutionize the membership experience when I worked in fitness, but I wasn't celebrated for it. Since leaving the industry, I have seen what I pioneered being done in other gyms and fitness studios. It makes me smirk because I know where it all came from. Only I know that it was born from years of watching my colleagues attempt to one-up each other. The never-ending battle among them was to earn a place in the spotlight and a chance to move up the company ladder.

My creations also came from enduring endless, *"How come you're so quiet?"* questions after monthly manager meetings. I never did tell any of them that I was quiet because I was paying close attention and taking copious notes of each of their successes and failures.

I was invested in my career and always implemented what I had learned for the benefit of the company, but I was made to feel as though I wasn't enough. I didn't speak up enough, wasn't talkative enough, engaged enough, or nice enough. I even had a boss tell me when I wasn't getting the promotion I thought I was, *"You're not loud enough, your voice just isn't heard, you've got to be more assertive."* Yes, he said all of that in one sentence.

No employer ever saw me. Instead, I was used, insulted, passed up for promotions, betrayed, and lied to. Many years of my life were spent reading books recommended by others to become the type of person they believed was ideal—charismatic, persuasive, and the life of the party. Despite the number of books I read, not only did I not become any of those things, but I had no desire to be.

What I did desire was to be **me**. I longed to do things my way and be celebrated for it, much as Meryl had been. I wanted to be quiet, listen, observe, and contemplate the best response in a hundred different ways before speaking or acting. I wanted more than anything to have the freedom to process information adequately and not stumble over my words in front of a group of people. I didn't want to force myself into conversations, but be invited in. I desperately wanted people to understand that it's never about me having nothing to say! I just need a freaking minute!

I'm a believer that there are no coincidences in life. There is a reason why I tuned in to the *Golden Globe Awards* that night in time to catch that presentation. It was the little seed that was planted in my head that led me to dive deeper into discovering what Introversion was. It gave me that little bit of inspiration that maybe I could be as brilliant as Meryl Streep. I began to fantasize about surrounding myself with people who understood me and celebrated me for the ways in which I was unique. Maybe I could also lean into my uniqueness instead of running from it. Maybe then I could actually have the impact on the world I deeply desired.

> "Being different isn't a bad thing. It means you're brave enough
> to be yourself." — Luna Lovegood

The desire to leave my "9-5" where I was never "enough" grew stronger as I decided I didn't want to mask who I was to fit in. Starting my own business allowed me to sort out who I was, and who I wasn't, without a boss telling me who I "should" be. This is not to say that the array of coaching programs I invested in along the way to help me with my business didn't perpetuate the "Extrovert Ideal."

In the online entrepreneur space, the extrovert personality is still heavily favored. The bold, charismatic hustlers are the ones destined to be ultra-successful, while the quiet, contemplative creatives are the ones needing transformation.

I did eventually come to the realization that I got to decide what was true in my business, and I happily called bullshit.

There is a smile breaking through as I write these words because I can honestly say that I've embraced who I am, once and for all. After years of feeling as though something was wrong with me, after hearing I wasn't "ideal" more times than I can begin to count, I have finally quit trying to make anyone other than myself approve of who I am. Today, I am brave enough to be myself. But, I'm sure you're wondering *"How?"* The secret for me was to reconnect with my childhood passions. It was therapeutic and the escape I needed to reset my conditioning.

Instead of pushing through weekends, striking up conversations, and getting sales appointments, I spent them in bookstores and exploring new destinations. Doing this forced me to remember who I was, what brought me joy, and what I was good at. It provided me with unwavering strength and bravery to say, *"This is me, this the real f—ing Jenny!"* It ignited my inspiration!

As a result of embracing my unique set of strengths, traits, and passions, the path I was meant to walk in this life came sharply into focus. With clarity and inspiration came a flood of ideas and a newfound sense of possibility, not only for myself but for other women just like me. I asked myself, *So what if I prefer to communicate in writing rather than speaking?* Then affirmed, *This isn't a weakness. This isn't something I need to fix. This is a strength! I need to lean into it.* And so I did, unapologetically.

Introvert, She Wrote Publishing was born to provide a platform for the quieter, more reserved female entrepreneurs to get massive visibility on their terms. It is a publishing company for every woman who has been made to feel that, in order to be taken seriously, she needs to be loud or even aggressive. We're removing the narrative of "gregarious means successful" and replacing it with "authenticity is ideal."

I want to leave you with these three truths:

1. You deserve to experience life through your own lens

- You are one of one, gorgeous. You were born totally unique from anyone else who's ever been on this Earth. You deserve to be that person completely! Claim that because it is yours. Otherwise, you end up cheating yourself out of the unique experience you are intended to have.

2. Lean into your natural strengths

- Whatever you are already good at, whatever comes easy, do those things and commit to being better at them. There is a reason you've been gifted your set of strengths. To use them! The world does a good job of making you think that you need to constantly fix your weaknesses. It's not true. While I am not suggesting you don't improve yourself, I'm saying don't forget you have infinite internal magic to tap into.

3. It's OK to do things that make your soul happy

- Not only is it OK, but I would highly encourage you to intentionally spend time doing things that make you fiercely happy. You will reconnect with your inner child and they will help you embrace all of your uniquenesses with grace and compassion.

ABOUT JENNY

Jenny Alberti is the CEO of Introvert, She Wrote Publishing, co-founder of the Women Writing Intentionally Collective, and an international Best-Selling Author. She helps Female Visionaries lean into their personality and leverage their strengths.

Jenny believes that remaining in alignment with and celebrating who we are is essential to fulfillment in business and life. She emboldens her authors to show up as their unique selves, communicate their valuable message with the world, and get paid for their gifts.

Through her solo and multi-author book containers, Jenny intends to shift the paradigm around visibility for female entrepreneurs. It is her dominant intent to help amplify the voices of all women who are here to make an epic impact on the world.

Jenny loves traveling and discovering new places. She plans to travel more with her incredible partner in the coming years.

Connect with Jenny:

10

KELLY VANHOVELN

PERFECTLY MADE

I was three-years-old the first time I realized there was something wrong with me. My parents had taken me to a birthday party but, although excited to play with the other kids, within minutes of our arrival I dissolved into a clingy, crying toddler who needed her daddy.

What I can articulate now, but couldn't then, is that it was overwhelming to me; the unfamiliar house, the noise of so many people, the in-your-face nature of the birthday girl as soon as we walked in the door.

While I warmed up to the environment and eventually gravitated towards the other kids, I remember sucking my thumb and clinging to my dad's leg, wishing I were more like the gregarious birthday girl.

If you are an introvert, or highly-sensitive person, my guess is that you, too, have experienced the shame of not being "normal", or had the desire to be more outgoing, fun-loving, and spontaneous. My story today is for you.

I want you to know that there is nothing wrong with you. You are perfectly made, exactly who you are meant to be, and you can do great things without changing yourself.

This has been a hard-learned lesson for me. I can recount dozens of times during the two decades following the birthday party where I wished I was different:

- While the rest of my scout troop excitedly ran to the swirly slides and the high dive, I preferred to play it safe in the lazy river.

- When the cast and crew of the school play planned an epic after-party, I was secretly relieved that my early curfew meant I'd have to go home and listen to music alone instead.

- When a cute upperclassman made a joke at my expense and the other girls in my dorm had to coach me through a flirty response for the next time because, that first time, I just turned red and walked away in tears.

That constant feeling of not fitting in, feeling shameful, and believing I was broken persisted for years.

During my mid-twenties, I got married and had my first daughter, and suddenly found myself in a joyful season as a stay-at-home-mom. While the hours were crummy and the boss, my infant daughter, was very demanding, I found peace in being home alone all day with her.

And, while other moms in my circle complained of the isolation and going crazy from being home all day, I fell in love with taking my daughter on long walks, quiet afternoons at the park, and luxurious nap times where I could read, journal and care for myself.

This was when I first realized that maybe there wasn't anything wrong with me but that, simply, I was wired differently.

It wasn't until I was in my thirties, when I was again feeling broken, that I finally discovered introversion.

In order for me to be a stay-at-home mom all those years, I had to find a way to bring in a couple of hundred dollars each week. For a while, I ran an in-home daycare, watching just one or two kids at a time. When I became pregnant with my second daughter, the stress of watching other people's kids became too much, and I knew I had to find something different.

One weekend, after a burst of inspiration, I typed up and sent out letters to fifty small businesses in my town, offering general office help. While the term "Virtual Assistant" hadn't yet been invented, that's essentially what I offered.

From those fifty, one lovely boutique owner offered me something that sparked what, over the next ten years, would grow to become a life-changing business. Sharon hired me to write blog posts about new arrivals in her boutique and share the posts online. She'd heard that a thing called "social media" was becoming a great place to spread the word about your business in the online world, and she was ready to test it for herself.

It turned out that I had a real knack for social media. I loved writing catchy content and exploring the reaches of *Twitter* and *Facebook* to network with other businesses in our area. The adrenaline hit I got when someone commented or shared one of our posts was truly addictive.

I loved that I could put my girls down for their naps, sit in front of the computer and, for two hours, write, read, engage, and interact from the comfort of my own bedroom. I was making a difference and making decent money, with no real "peopling" required.

For the next seven years, I freelanced, taking on clients here and there and working with only a handful of hours each week. My business grew through word-of-mouth and I loved every second. It allowed me to stay home with all of my kids until first grade, (my son came along a couple of years after my younger daughter), and, just a few years ago when the kids were all in school full-time, I decided to take my nice little side gig and turn it into a full-time operation.

While I knew nothing about running a business, I loved digital marketing and I truly wanted to help other business owners find success on social media. I hoped that would be enough.

In early 2019, I committed myself to entrepreneurship, and set my sights on hitting six figures in my business within two years. After a few months, I was having some success; I'd signed a few clients for tiny projects by responding to job posts in *Facebook* groups, but I felt lost.

The online entrepreneurship world was more cutthroat than I ever imagined it would be. I just wanted to help people but, everywhere I looked, other social media managers had better websites, better graphics, more salesy-sounding pitches, and higher incomes. I knew I needed to get better at selling my services, but I didn't know where to start.

In what turned out to be a twist of fate, a client of mine had recently found a business coach who helped female entrepreneurs grow their businesses. Steph promised that she could guide me to that six-figure business I dreamed of in just a few months, as long as I was willing to follow her plan and work hard.

The first red flag should have been the way she manipulated me on our sales call, letting me sob for nearly two hours about how desperate I was for success, but I thought that's how sales had to be done. She said all the right things, made all the right promises, and I found myself committing to paying her $20k over the next year to guide me on my journey.

Two sessions into our contract, she gave me an assignment that turned my stomach and made my skin crawl: compile a list of a hundred businesses in my area who might want my services and cold-call them that week. I'd be pitching a $3000/month social media package to complete strangers.

As most introverts know, phone calls are a special form of torture. There's no telling who might be on the other end of the phone, there's no body language to help you decipher what's being said between the lines, and you have to think of the next thing to say on the fly. No amount of planning can prepare you for every single direction a conversation might take.

Cold-calling nearly killed my entrepreneurial dreams. What my coach expected me to complete in one week that summer, I dragged out to nearly two months. I could get through five calls a day before the anxiety became so intense that I needed to vomit.

I'd spend hours crying after completing the calls, beating myself up for being so scared, so desperate, so uncomfortable with what I thought was the only way to grow a profitable business.

When I met with my coach, her "help" only confirmed what I already knew; I was broken, damaged goods, too quiet to ever succeed in business.

"You're just going to need to power through."

"You're too worried about what they'll think of you."

"You need to be more aggressive."

"It's just business."

For the next year, I spun in circles with my coach as she recommended one slimy, pushy sales tactic after another, and I tried each of them for a couple of weeks, only to fail and further confirm to myself that I was not the type of person who could succeed in business. Every phone call, email, sales push, "launch", and bait-n-switch tactic left me feeling like a con artist, killed my confidence, and pushed me deeper into a depression.

Luckily, in August 2020, God stepped in and changed everything.

A derecho blew through my state, leaving a path of destruction in its wake. Our county had no power, no internet, and no phone lines for over two weeks. While I was initially in a panic about my business, after a few days, I realized that time was a gift. With no way to contact the outside world, I was left with plenty of brain space to think about business-building on my own terms. I used that time to sift through the advice of my coach and get clear on my priorities.

More than anything, I wanted to operate from a place of integrity. While I wanted to be paid well for my work, I also truly wanted to help people. I knew I had a special skill set that tons of businesses needed, but hustling to convince people to work with me just wasn't working *for* me.

Here's what I've learned about introversion. Our brain's reaction to dopamine is thought to be the mechanism that drives many of the characteristics of the introverted brain—deep thinking, feeling drained by social situations, aversion to risk, and being highly self-aware. Understanding how this mechanism works, and how to work *with* it rather than against it, means a more joyful, calm, and contented existence for us introverts.

A lot of us know dopamine as the "reward" chemical or the "pleasure neu-rotransmitter," but it's really the motivation neurotransmitter. We get a hit of dopamine both from the *anticipation* of a job well done (have you ever committed to a big life change and felt a bit of a buzz before you even got started?) and from the *completion* of a job well done.

Dopamine helps ALL of us, introvert or not, to pursue our goals and make things happen. In many people, the dopamine hit from a "win" triggers a feeling of joy or euphoria but, in introverts, that second, more intense hit can be overwhelming and overstimulating. So rather than pursue it, we avoid it.

This is why we avoid social interaction; it gives us a too-intense hit of dopamine. It's why we're risk-averse; risky behavior promotes big wins, which means an enormous hit of dopamine. It's why we love deep-thinking and we're self-aware; by constantly analyzing things and paying attention to our inner state, we avoid doing activities that overwhelm us.

In a culture that rewards extroverted behavior, we can often feel like outcasts. The truth is that our introverted nature is a huge boon to our ability to grow a successful business.

- We're wired for pursing the long-game, meaning that when our business isn't an overnight success, we don't give up.

- We keep at it, a little at a time, until we gradually build success.

- We're wired for deep relationships, which means that we don't make promises we can't keep.

- We operate from deep integrity, and focus on what's truly best for our clients and their successes.

- We're wired for strategic action, so we don't take unnecessary risks in business.

- We approach every stage of growth with a clear plan for how to achieve our next goal.

We introverts are designed to achieve great things when we harness the power of the unique chemistry in our brains. Back then, all I knew was that I couldn't hustle anymore. I needed to do business MY way.

At the end of my two-week natural-disaster induced hiatus, I'd developed a plan to find clients for my social media business using, of all things, social media. While the exact strategies have changed over the years, there are three rules that continue to serve as a guiding light for everything I do:

1. Build real relationships

2. Focus on the needs of your clients

3. Sell in a way that plays to your strengths

With those three rules in place, I developed a plan to build an audience of people who would truly benefit from my help. With no room for cold-calling or spammy emails, I targeted each communication precisely to the needs of my target audience and gently nudged them into my marketing ecosystem through valuable content, deep insight, and low-stakes calls-to-action.

I reached out to individual business owners within my audience each week, checking in to see how business was, offering a few simple takeaways they could implement right away, and then following up to ask how things were going. Only when one would admit, *"I just can't do this myself,"* would I offer my services.

My approach was not an overnight-success type of situation. There were no *"10k in 10 days"* miracles or ground-breaking revenue months, but it worked. Within a few months, I had signed three new clients into retainer packages and was sitting comfortably at an income level just higher than what I'd made when I was working full time.

I was operating in full integrity, had great relationships with my clients, and I knew every one of them truly valued the work I was doing for them.

I wish I could say that I was content at this point. Content to let myself settle into the rhythm of having a handful of clients on my roster. Content to earn what was truly great income. Content to sit back and admire what I'd built, totally on my own, in a way that simply felt right, in only a few months.

As always, there was a voice in my head telling me that I was broken. I felt like a fraud. I was afraid that, because I hadn't done it the "real" way, because I'd slowly built real relationships and relied on comfortable ways of networking, that my business wasn't good enough. That I wasn't good enough.

Even after all this time, I still couldn't escape the feeling of being damaged goods.

Thankfully, the magic of the algorithm saved me. One day, an intriguing article about the unique strengths of the introvert popped up in my suggestions. I devoured the article, nodding my head in agreement as every point hit home:

- I love writing (my love for social media!)

- I prefer to be alone (my love of working from home!)

- I value deep relationships (my marketing plan is based on real conversations!)

- I operate out of integrity (my desire to truly help my clients!)

- I could see the long game (my need to have a solid plan that took time to implement!)

As the pieces clicked into place, the weight lifted. Not only was I not damaged or broken, but there was a truly scientific reason that I couldn't follow the hustle-based, *"go for no,"* slimy sales plan my coach (and, truly, the entire online business culture) pushed on me; my brain is wired differently.

Today, I no longer wonder what's wrong with me. I do not consider myself "damaged goods." I've embraced introversion and the limitations and the strengths that come with it. Shortly after I discovered introversion, I began to notice how many other women there were just like me in the online entrepreneurial space. I'd often see a dozen threads a day talking about business strategy or social media platforms and, inevitably, there would be comments like:

"It's only extroverts who make that kind of money."

"I'm too quiet to use social media."

"I suck at sales because I'm an introvert."

"How can I be more extroverted?"

While my heart breaks for these women, their struggles have lit a fire in me to change the online business world, one introverted woman at a time.

Here's what I want you to know. You can operate from complete integrity, make a massive impact in your clients' lives, and get paid amazingly well when you show up authentically as the quiet badass you are.

ABOUT KELLY

 Kelly VanHoveln wants you to know that you are amazing just the way you are. She knows you can grow your business and make good money in a way that works with your strengths as an introverted, sensitive, or shy person.

After fourteen years in the online world, Kelly has developed unique strategies for marketing and selling online. Through her podcast "The Social-Savvy Introvert," her Facebook™ Group of the same name, and her 1:1 coaching, she now teaches introverted coaches how to create and sell to audiences full of people who hang onto their every word, by taking strategic actions and stepping into their role as thought leaders in their industry.

Kelly lives in an introvert's paradise—a 5-acre wooded property in the middle-of-nowhere, Iowa with her husband, three kids, and an assortment of feathered and furry friends.

Connect with Kelly:

11

LIZ MEDFORD

THE PROBLEM WITH PERFECTIONISM

To put yourself out there as an introvert is a scary thing. Being *badass* means that I can "feel the fear and do it anyway" and, so, I share with you how my breakdown became my breakthrough.

I used to think I had to be perfect. A star student, with straight-A's from elementary school through grad school, I graduated valedictorian, attended college on a full scholarship, and got into an Ivy League master's program. Just like a movie, I married my high-school sweetheart, who was also the captain of the football team. I landed nearly every job I ever applied for and started a PhD with the most famous professor in my field. But, despite my external successes, I never felt happy. I constantly overworked, felt incredibly lonely and, at my worst, I wanted to die.

I vividly remember the first time it happened.

One afternoon when I came home from high school, my mom handed me a letter from the advanced studies summer program I'd applied for. There was little doubt I'd be accepted - after all, I was ranked #1 in a class of 310. Excitedly, I tore open the letter to learn that, although I got into the program, I'd been assigned not to my first two course choices (marine biology or ecology), but to my third choice, engineering.

I broke into tears, ran down to the basement, locked the door, and tried to hang myself. When my dad broke down the door, I ran away.

My brain told me that if I wasn't good enough to get into my first choice, then I didn't deserve to be alive. (It didn't matter that my mom called the program the next day, and they switched me into my preferred subject.) The first of many visits to that dark place inside my head was a scary place to be.

My Fall from Grace

Many times, my perfectionism nearly killed me; and it always held me back.

As a perfectionist, I was hyper-sensitive to criticism, needed to control everyone and everything around me, and would either say no to opportunities that might be challenging, or walk away as soon as things got hard in order to avoid failure. Fast-forward twenty years and I had destroyed my marriage, dropped out of my PhD program, and was in survival mode, working my way through a series of short-term jobs in the years that followed my divorce. I'd taken up peak-bagging as a way to manage and distract from my loneliness and emotional pain.

Peak-bagging is the hobby of hiking every mountain on a list, usually all the peaks above a certain elevation in a particular region (e.g., the White Mountain 4,000-footers). My veil of perfection had been pierced too many times, and I thought if I could manage to climb the hundred highest New England peaks in winter—an elite feat limited to barely one hundred hikers, mostly men—I could restore some sense of personal achievement in the wake of all my recent failures.

The previous winter, I had finished hiking the *New England 67*, a list consisting of the sixty-seven peaks above 4,000 feet in New Hampshire, Maine, and Vermont. This left me thirty-three peaks just under 4,000 feet to climb in the twelve weeks between the Winter Solstice and the Spring Equinox, many of which were trailless bushwhacks located down unplowed logging roads.

Winter hiking alone is unsafe and breaking trail through several feet of fresh snow is best done in groups, so I connected online with others who were working towards this goal and joined forces on the most difficult hikes.

With the entire winter planned out, I knew exactly which peaks I needed to hike, on which weekends, in order to reach my goal by March. Until the unexpected happened.

Frigid temperatures and heavy snowfall ahead of one of the most remote hikes of the season caused my hiking partners to cancel. Without their backcountry cabin reservation and help to break trail, I couldn't attempt this hike. And I knew if I didn't get those two peaks that particular weekend, I wouldn't be able to finish the list that season. Rage bubbled up towards these people who had ruined my plans, even though I knew the conditions were marginal at best.

Alone at home, I screamed and cried. I could not handle the fact that I wouldn't be able to complete my goal as planned. My life felt like it was unraveling. Something inside me snapped.

On Monday morning, I wandered into my shared office muttering under my breath in front of a coworker that I wanted to die. My peak-bagging goal was the only thing moving me forward in life and, if I didn't have that, my brain thought there was nothing left to live for. My boss overheard my frightening words, called me into her office and, after I unloaded on her about what a bad place I was in, I negotiated to take a couple of months off to pursue mental health treatment. That was the last time I had a full-time job.

I spent most of the next year and a half in bed and in therapy, trying to navigate the social services network of disability, Medicaid, and food stamps to keep me alive.

The Problem with Perfectionism

As a perfectionist and over-achiever, to go from top of my class to unemployed and dependent on government aid created a profound identity crisis for me. Yet, it was also the beginning of my healing journey.

The problem with perfectionism is that it makes our self-worth contingent on our flawless achievement. I believed that I was only good enough if I was the best. My perfectionist parts thought that if I never made a mistake, I would never have to face the pain of criticism or judgment from others. And, because I got so used to NOT making mistakes and NOT being second best, I never developed the resilience to learn and grow. Instead, I was afraid to try new things if I didn't know that I would instantly be good at them and I walked away from opportunities as soon as I started to struggle.

In that reality, it was more important to me to maintain the outward illusion of perfection to others than it was to persevere and risk failure in the pursuit of my dreams. But that black-and-white thinking led me to a place of profound darkness when this series of setbacks caused me to give up entirely—on my goals, and almost on my life.

Perfectionism is commonly misunderstood as being detail-oriented and striving for excellence, but there is an important distinction between perfectionism and excellence. Striving to do good work is healthy. Basing one's value and self-worth on an ideal of perfection, and punishing oneself for falling short, is pathological. When perfection is the ideal, the end result is inevitable disappointment.

For most of my life, I had mistakenly taken pride in my perfectionist streak, thinking that achievement was the path to happiness and acceptance. The unraveling of my life around me forced a reckoning, and I finally saw that striving for perfection was destroying me.

My Road to Recovery

I had to face the fact that this perfectionist coping strategy I'd followed my whole life was no longer working. I was diagnosed with an alphabet soup of psychiatric disorders, from anxiety and depression to BPD and PTSD, and was eventually approved (through a lengthy bureaucratic process) for disability because I was unable to go back to work. The first year-and-a-half following my breakdown was spent in almost daily medical appointments, individual and group therapy sessions, and twelve-step meetings.

Thankfully, I quit drinking when I realized that alcohol fueled my self-destructive behavior. As a result of these diagnoses, I was prescribed about fifteen different psychiatric medications over the course of the next few years, none of which seemed to help. I discovered Dialectical Behavior Therapy (DBT) and completed a nine-month online program as well as a two-week residential treatment program to gain new skills.

There were many ups and downs during this process, but I slowly started to rebuild my life. I reconnected with a childhood sweetheart who became my second husband and, together we finished what I'd started. He stood beside me on a zero-degree day in the middle of an epic twenty-mile winter hike when I finished my final peak for the *New England Hundred Highest* list.

About a year-and-a-half into my recovery, I started to feel well enough to explore what was next. Aware that going back to work full-time for an employer would jeopardize my mental health, and eager to use my new tools to help others, I began to explore the possibility of working for myself and creating a career where I could help people while also taking care of myself.

One of my mentors during my recovery was a life coach whose story was similar to mine; she'd had a mental health breakdown and used her recovery to help others. Around the same time, I joined a program to learn about entrepreneurship and met another woman training to be a life coach. I realized this could be a great path for me to help people and, within a matter of weeks, I was enrolled in a two-year life coach certification program.

Discovering my Parts

My biggest breakthrough came during a weekend of life coach training. In a conference room at a fancy hotel in downtown Boston, with floor-to-ceiling windows facing views of skyscrapers and city streets, I sat with my twenty classmates in a semi-circle of chairs facing our instructor at the front of the room. I'd kept quiet for most of the weekend, too afraid to volunteer for a demonstration or answer questions.

Perfectionism fueled my inner introvert; if I wasn't 100% sure I'd say the right thing, I couldn't speak at all. I certainly wasn't expecting what came next when the instructor prompted us through an exercise to dig deep and uncover our biggest fear.

As I stared at the vines weaving their way through the carpet on the floor in front of me, I worked my way deeper into my psyche. With the instructor's prompts, when I peeled back the layers I was hiding behind, I discovered that my deepest fear was not being good enough. Suddenly it became clear to me why I'd been striving my whole life for the next accomplishment, the next achievement, and for being the best at everything I did. This was because even the slightest failure or mistake triggered this basic fear: *if I'm not the best, then at my core, I'm no good at all.*

We all have our own basic fear that drives us.

The more I delved into my coach training, the more I began to learn about different parts of me that were hard at work trying to protect me from facing my deepest fear. My Co-Active coach training introduced the idea that we have a part of us called a "Saboteur" that represents all the negative voices in our heads; it's the one that says *"I can't. What will people think? Nothing ever works out for me."* In Co-Active coaching, the antidote to the Saboteur is to side-step it with other parts called "Allies" that have our best interest at heart, and by channeling our "Inner Leader", the wise true self who guides us.

The idea that I had different parts at work inside my brain resonated deeply; I could notice a palpable shift in energy when my Saboteur took over, like a dark cloud rolling in and obscuring the sun. I also began to identify different inner Allies like my playful part that loves to laugh and be silly, my badass part that can propel me up and down mountains, and my teacher part that switches on when I need to explain something.

A little over a year into my coach training, I discovered *Positive Intelligence*, a book by Shirzad Chamine that revealed that we can have as many as ten different saboteurs inside our heads, as well as the wise inner guide that he calls our "Sage." Shirzad's book identifies an array of saboteurs including our inner "Judge, Avoider, Stickler, Pleaser, Hyper-Achiever, Controller, Hyper-Vigilant, Restless, Hyper-Rational, and Victim."

In 2020, I had the opportunity to be a part of the very first cohort of coaches to train with Shirzad to become a *Certified Positive Intelligence Coach* (CPQC). I had just completed my *Certified Professional Co-Active Coach* (CPCC) program, and *Positive Intelligence* gave me a new set of tools I could use to help people understand and interrupt their patterns of self-sabotage. I was already working with clients one-on-one as a life coach, and I launched a group program and membership to further support people in learning the tools of PQ.

Around the same time, I discovered an even more in-depth model of parts-work called *Internal Family Systems* (IFS), developed by Richard Schwartz. IFS gave me a more nuanced understanding of the parts-work model. What my Co-Active and PQ training dubbed "Saboteurs" were known as "Protectors" in the IFS model, the parts of our personality that developed at a young age to protect us from emotional pain. IFS holds that these parts are not our enemies, even though their actions can cause us a lot of stress and unhappiness. Their role is to protect our young, vulnerable, inner-child parts, called "Exiles," from experiences that trigger deep emotional pain (which is rooted in past trauma).

Suddenly, it all made sense! My inner perfectionist had been working on overdrive my whole life to protect the little girl inside of me from feeling the pain of not being good enough. IFS theory held that if I could heal the exiled little girl from her emotional pain, and help her embrace all of her beautiful child-like qualities, then my Protector parts could let go of their extreme roles and become more functional parts of my internal family.

I have had the honor of guiding clients through this powerful process, and I work with my own IFS practitioner to heal the parts of me that experienced childhood trauma and redirect the perfectionist parts that have been working so hard to protect me.

Embracing UNperfectionism

In the midst of this self-discovery, born from a place of desperation, I created my concept of *UNperfectionism*.

Less than a year into my coaching business, I almost gave up. After working hard for many months to build a website and *Facebook* group, attend networking events, write blogs, and post on social media, six months into my entrepreneurial journey, I had just one client. I spiraled again and made this mean that I was no good, that no one wanted to work with me, so why bother? Back to the emptiness of feeling like a failure, I tried to figure out what was next because, deep down, I knew I wasn't ready to quit.

This was before I'd cultivated my full coaching toolkit but, even then, I recognized that my mindset was self-sabotaging me. That, once again, perfectionism was holding me back, telling me that because I didn't immediately succeed at entrepreneurship, I was a failure and might as well give up. And something in me realized, perhaps for the first time, that failing did NOT mean I was no good and should quit. It just meant that I needed to try again; to learn from what didn't work and do something different.

My head started buzzing with ideas and inspiration as I stayed up all night searching for the right domain name to build a brand that would help other people let go of perfectionism, so they could lead happier, more fulfilling lives.

In this flurry of inspiration, *UNperfectionism* was born from the mantra that accepting our "imperfections" is not enough; we need to outright reject perfection as the ideal and undo our perfectionist conditioning by celebrating our failures, giving ourselves permission to do B-level work, and loving ourselves for who we are, not what we do.

UNperfectionism is so much more liberating than perfectionism!

UNperfectionism leads to personal growth because trying something and iterating is how we grow.

UNperfectionism makes us more relatable. Who wants to hang out with someone who is so flawless and thinks they are better than everyone else?

UNperfectionism is a lot more fun! You get to do what you want, how you want. You stop worrying about what is the "right" way and lean into what is your way.

UNperfectionism is badass because you don't care what other people think of you or what is "right". There is boldness in being yourself and doing what lights you up.

UNperfectionism is how I finally overcame my fear of writing. The thinking that I could only "be a writer" if I adhered to some canonical rules of perfection. It allowed me to contribute to this book and become a published author.

I have embraced my uniqueness by turning my mission to overcome perfectionism into a business. I've had the privilege of helping dozens of women through my coaching programs at UNperfectionism.com—my Badass Business Bootcamp for entrepreneurs, and my mindset coaching focused on parts-work.

I have a variety of free trainings and resources available at UNperfectionism.com/free, and I'll be launching my UNperfectionism podcast this year! To me, epic impact is not just changing one life, but having an impact on others in a way that allows them to also change the lives of those around them.

Letting go of perfectionism is the most badass thing I've ever done. It's badass because it's scary. It requires overcoming the fear of failure, fear of criticism, fear of judgment, and fear of rejection. And it is a lifelong journey. But the reward is to become the person you are meant to be—in all your UNperfect uniqueness!

About Liz

Liz Medford is a Mindset Coach, Business Strategist, and Founder of UNperfectionism .com and the Badass Business Bootcamp. She helps women pursue their passions without getting stuck in perfectionism, procrastination, and overwhelm.

Liz holds space for her clients to do deep mindset work, uncovering the parts of themselves that are holding them back and cultivating their inner sense of self to guide them toward their goals. She has been featured as a guest expert for the Center for Women and Enterprise, the Women's Rural Entrepreneurial Network, the Hannah Grimes Center for Entrepreneurship, and She Built This.

Liz is a Certified Professional Co-Active Coach (CPCC), a Certified Positive Intelligence Coach (CPQC), and an Internal Family Systems (IFS) parts work practitioner. She holds a master's degree from Yale University. Liz lives in the White Mountains of New Hampshire and has hiked the hundred highest peaks in New England, twice.

Connect with Liz:

12

NICOLE RICHARDS

THE WARRIOR IS AWAKE

I 'm an expert at many things. My biggest expertise? Well, over the years, I've become a top expert at hiding; fitting into whatever mold was required. Being adaptable, staying behind the scenes, not wanting to be seen or heard, keeping my voice as small as possible, so I don't rock the boat and stand out.

Standing out was too much attention, too loud, and the feeling of being "too naked," even with my clothes on.

I was encouraged to live this life as a child. To speak when spoken to, have fewer big ideas, to just follow along. As I moved into adulthood, I crafted a fantastic career as a makeup artist, designed away from the spotlight, just the way I liked it. I believe my friends and colleagues would describe me as a badass based on my accomplishments. But quiet? They wouldn't describe me that way. Let me explain.

Born a warrior, I was bold, curious, and outspoken. I'm at ease in highly interactive social situations, so "introvert" wasn't a label for me. Introverts are often described as people who like to keep to themselves, but that blanket description doesn't fit everyone. With more understanding, I would eventually call myself an 'extroverted-introvert.' Drop me in a room with 200 people and I'll happily make friends by the end of the event.

The consequence of interacting on that energetic level? A weekend long 'nap' to recover from that output of energy, a foggy mind the next day, and a body that couldn't move more than an inch without feeling drained.

But can I tell you a secret? As much as I like meeting new people, sometimes I'm secretly happy when plans are canceled. Have you been there? Wanting to go out with friends but secretly hoping it's rescheduled? This thought wasn't coming from a place of negative energy but, sometimes, the mental capacity needed was too much, and I preferred to stay home in peace and quiet.

How would you describe a warrior? In movies, the warrior usually rides on horseback, with a shield and a sword, demanding to be seen and heard. Today, warriors could be a part of the military, nurses, or police officers, but there is also a quiet warrior who is often overlooked. One armed with the boldness and wisdom that allows discernment before taking action.

The modern quiet warrior uses their voice and experience to fight battles that effect change. No blood or guts required.

Fighting Inner Conflict

Have you ever wanted to disappear? When I was eight years old, I had a moment of terror with only one wish after giving a speech about squirrels in my third-grade class. A worthy topic that I thought was highly engaging, except I didn't fully understand public speaking and the concept of practicing consistently. Since my primary goal was not to die in front of my class, disappearing was the next best possibility.

I stood there, naked again, my little hands trembling, holding my cue cards tight so I didn't drop them, as I spoke in a low yet fast voice, trying to get it over with so I could run back to the safety of my seat. I vowed never, ever to do something like this again.

Fast forward to age thirteen when I did something I promised my eight-year-old self I'd never do! During music class, our teacher, Mrs. Bryan, was excited to announce our school would be putting on a play, *The Wizard of Oz*! Despite my promise, when it became clear that all my friends were auditioning, I didn't want to be left out, so I practiced and practiced.

When it was my turn to audition, the gym became a scary place. I had to sing *Somewhere Over the Rainbow* on the big stage, alone, with my classmates and a few other teachers waiting for the first note. I memorized the song so my hands could stay tightly clasped together as I worked through my nerves. Not knowing where to look, I focused on Mrs. Bryan.

As we held our gaze, I started off with a low tone. Mrs. Bryan began to mouth the words along with me, encouraging me with her eyes, and using her hands to move to the music. My voice became stronger and louder; the butterflies melted away. There was no microphone, so I had to project my voice. I felt my body move into the song. I was having a great time!

Of course, I wanted to be Dorothy but ended up being the Scarecrow—you know, the one without a brain? I was secretly happy the entire play didn't revolve around my part, but at the same time, sad I wasn't the main character.

At the end, I was pleasantly surprised when Mrs. Bryan exclaimed how much she loved my voice. I had no clue I could sing.

Unaware that anyone would enjoy my singing voice, when I got a standing ovation the night of the play, I learned I had a superpower. I could be seen and heard. People listened instead of casting judgment about my abilities. My eight-year-old self was cheering me on in the background and super proud of me.

My Life's Biggest Inner Conflict

The introvert in me needed to embrace the gifts and talents of the extroverted side, but I couldn't get them to agree. I began to sing at talent shows but I wasn't comfortable hearing my voice in a microphone and my hand shook when I held one so I had to use the mic stand.

I couldn't get over that inability to have all eyes on me and be comfortable on stage so, eventually, I stopped doing an activity I really enjoyed. I slowly quieted my voice and talent, refrained from being "big" to avoid the feelings that I was being judged, but God had other plans.

What happens when the warrior forgets how powerful she is? Who does she become? When a warrior forgets her power, she becomes molded into whoever the surrounding people think she should be. She isn't speaking *her* truth enough, so others seem to create an impression for her.

What happens when society gets a hold of a child who won't conform and is a bold, free-spirited thinker? When teachers, and later employers, believe that this quiet genius isn't participating at the level they believe is necessary, the warrior becomes outnumbered in battle and is verbally and mentally "beaten" into submission because she doesn't think like those who choose to live inside their own self-imposed box.

I was born a warrior but, as a child, that boldness wasn't allowed. My ideas and curiosity were diverted and shelved by adults around me. I became a quiet warrior. My passions and creativity burned inside me, unable to be free and shared without judgment.

I was born a warrior, but grew up in an era when children were to be seen and not heard. If you didn't have the right answers in school, the teacher would choose someone else who was louder and more expressive. Remember the saying, "The squeaky wheel gets the grease?" Louder and more bold, they labeled those students as "the ones who would go far in life."

I was born a warrior, but teachers, preachers, employers, and family quashed that inner drive. That part of me learning to be comfortable with my voice was constantly challenged and undermined, so I slowly stopped expressing my thoughts out loud. It was easier to be quiet, to say and do what's necessary to make everyone else feel comfortable. I bought into the idea that my voice and ideas were not valuable and not needed if I wasn't as expressive as everyone else.

The Truth about Mediocrity

When you fight to keep your limitations, you languish in mediocrity. I call this *living in the middle*. What's life like living in the middle? You're not at the bottom, but you're barely thriving, more concerned with the opinions of others, not living out your deepest potential. As we age, it's comfortable being there and little to no one has any expectations of you.

Being quiet and badass has some women *living in the middle*. Powerful and unique, yet someone or something has caused them to "quiet down." I lived here for way too long, minimizing my gifts and talents to make others feel comfortable. Until one day I said, *Enough!* and my warrior awakened.

There is Power in being Quietly Underestimated

Being quiet is a part of our warrior nature. The warrior has wisdom to survey the battlefield before jumping in blindly. We aren't always in action mode and need time to observe, recharge, strategize, and just be. Sometimes there's nothing to say, other times we just need to be present. People don't always understand our need to be quiet and observe.

In 2006, three weeks before marrying my highschool sweetheart, I got a fancy job in the glamorous area of Yorkville in Toronto, Ontario, Canada with one of the biggest cosmetic companies in the world. My role as an *Education Executive* was exciting and full of constantly moving parts. I felt highly unqualified for the job, but sometimes God blesses us with bigger responsibilities so we can stretch and grow. I grew and stretched more than a pair of spandex leggings three sizes too small!

I often stayed in observation mode, while my colleagues worked hard to impress their bosses with their words. There were times the extroverted part of me was just tired and the introvert took over. I found it exhausting to continually find creative ways to blow smoke up their butts, just to have something to contribute.

A few years into my new role, we traveled to California for a company conference in a stunning, no expense spared, five-star hotel resort. At the end of the conference, while waiting for our taxis to the airport, my Account Executive partners pressed me to debrief our next moves after the conference.

Drained, but on a great high after three days of learning, decadent meals, and excitement, I felt it was best to take time to process the conference notes and then make plans to discuss our strategy when we were back in Toronto.

I can thank my former personal trainer, Rita, for the strength I found at this moment. She'd been kicking my butt at 5:30am for six weeks, and I was feeling strong and sure of myself.

Since they outnumbered me, I usually gave in but, this time, the more they insisted, collectively, to have their way, the more I held my ground without batting an eyelash.

Quiet warriors weren't created to live a life *in the middle*. When we don't speak up, allow others to speak over us, or act upon preconceived notions, the real you is minimized. I politely recreated boundaries and maintained the expectation that those boundaries would be upheld. This was one of the most pivotal moments in my life. The warrior in me remembered I was just as powerful when I was quiet as I was when speaking up.

Months later, during a one-on-one meeting with my boss, she leaned in close and whispered, *"Your colleagues are intimidated by you. They say you never seem flustered."* That's what people see when you quietly observe and only speak when you have something real to say.

It was a confusing statement, but one I now understand; some can't handle the strength or power of a warrior, and I no longer choose to make that my concern.

The Silent War Within

In my last corporate job, my entire career was based around teaching, training, and being seen and heard. As an entrepreneur, I loved hosting events that gathered people together.

My soul desired to use my talents and potential to move into who God created me to be, but my mind kept telling me that being small was safer since I've lived that way my entire life. What other people thought of me became my focus instead of who I wanted to grow into.

Trying to live up to the expectations of who people think you are will drain you. When I gained my sense of power working for the cosmetic company, I was determined not to allow anyone to decide how big or small my voice should be.

For my own personal growth, I needed to resolve this inner conflict because I knew I had so much to offer, and worrying about what other people thought wasn't going to help me hit my life goals or reach those I wanted help.

Their Limitations are not Yours

In highschool, I booked my appointment with the guidance counselor and told her I wanted to do my community service at the biggest television station in Canada, *City TV*. They hosted *Fashion Television*, an international success, and I was willing to get as many cups of coffee as necessary just to be on set.

After excitedly explaining my big dream, she looked at me like I had asked her for a million dollars, then started laughing. Humiliated and angry, I was unable to speak up. At fifteen years old, I then believed it was too difficult and did my hours that semester at a daycare, then at a bank the following year where they used me as a free labored bank teller. I hated it and quit after two weeks.

Some twenty-five years later, I ran into my former highschool principal at *Staples*, the place all educators like to hang out. He didn't remember me, but I told him about my big dream and being "shut down" by the guidance counselor. Tall yet unintimidating, he looked visibly upset. I'll never forget his disappointed response, *"Your request wasn't crazy. We've done things like that in the past, but she probably didn't know how, so she dismissed the idea. Those were her limitations."*

At that point, I'd never put much thought into how much other people's limitations affect how we buy into our own. When the limitations and ideals of others become intertwined with our own subconscious, then you are at war within yourself.

Use your Superpowers

Over the years, it has become important to use my quietness as my greatest superpower, rather than my greatest weakness. My ability to read a room is one of the things that makes me badass and, as a result, I blossomed. The more I surveyed the adventure before jumping in, the better my opportunities became.

I was searching for the wells in my potential to see how far I could go, constantly, and sometimes not so quietly, pushing the envelope.

I'd love to say I'm always pressing through the feelings that come with introverted processing. There are times I'm proud I spoke up and days I'll kick myself for not being more assertive in specific situations.

What about You?

You're reading this book because the idea of being quiet and badass resonates with you. But are you leaning into being the badassery side of life and business? Or are you still leaning into living quietly under the radar?

Even though I don't know you, the fact that you're reading this book means you resonate with our stories and you seek to use your voice in a way that will help you grow you towards becoming your truest self.

I've included an exercise at the end of this chapter that will help you work through some questions and move through the fears that keep you feeling like your voice isn't big enough.

There is a version of yourself you haven't met yet. She's counting on you to show up in a bigger, yet authentic, way in your life. The version of 'you' five years from now is counting on today's version of you to use your quiet badass self to play a bigger game.

Other people's ideas about who you are, are no longer your concern. It's time to take inventory of the situations, experiences and voices that aren't your own yet have taken up residence in your subconscious, causing you to live a life in the middle, quiet and a little less badass.

Will you try an experiment with me?

My inner healing program www.thewarriorisawake.co will take you on a soul searching journey of inner reflection. The end goal is to forgive those who have underestimated you, and 'grow yourself up' into the next version of who you were meant to be.

When you join the program, you'll receive a notebook with 50+ questions. The goal is not a cramming session to answer all the questions. This inner work is meant to be done over a minimum of a month, but you can choose one question and work on it for a few days until you feel released from the question.

Here are four questions you can answer to propel you to becoming the newest version of yourself. A new person, unconcerned with other people's thoughts or impressions of you. This work is best done in solitude, with pen and paper, wrestling to birth the new version of yourself.

Get comfortable, turn off your phone, and begin by asking:

1. Who do I want to become while building this next level of me?

2. Who have I been in the old version of me?

3. Whose voice in my life has caused the most influence on building the old version of me?

4. How will I do the work to forgive them and remove their version of me from my life?

Once you've done this exercise, email me and let me know who you want to become in the new version of you? nr@nicolerichards.co

ABOUT NICOLE

 Nicole Richards is a Certified Life Coach and entrepreneur. A lifelong student of mindset renewal, human behavior, emotional resilience, and business strategy, she is also a woman of faith. Working with her is not for the faint of heart, as her goal is to find and pursue the depths of your God-given potential.

Nicole helps quiet dreamers create possibilities out of the impossible. The obstacles holding us back are valid, but it's time to write a better story.

By working on their thoughts and looking inward at their gifts and talents, Nicole guides her clients to create a new life and finish it well. Her secret sauce is seeing the greatness in others and pulling it into view so they can share it with the world.

Before becoming a life coach, Nicole was a published Master Airbrush Makeup Artist and producer who spent over twenty years creatively designing concepts to tell stories that sell. She lives near Toronto, Ontario, Canada with her children.

Connect with Nicole:

13

SIMONE JAMES

MY TIME TO FLOURISH

Everybody has a story to tell and, honestly, mine isn't special compared to 99% of the population but, to me, it represents the *Badass* person I have become. I could say, I am happy with who I am and there's nothing more I need to improve, but that's BS!

I look at who I am now and feel like a quiet, badass woman who's experienced many tribulations in life. Through these tribulations, I've come out the other side a strong, determined, loving person who knows what she wants and will do anything, within legal parameters, to get there.

When I think about how my eating disorder developed, my first memory goes back to when I was about six. My dad often came to my room to kiss me goodnight after work and sneak me a *Caramello* chocolate bar. Gosh, I loved those things! After he left, I'd roll over and eat that bar like my life depended on it, feeling incredibly happy and loved.

At thirteen, I sat in my room with chocolates sprawled out on the floor around me while I cried because the kids at school were cruel. I cried because they called me fat, ugly, and a loser. One by one, I started to eat those chocolates, my feelings of sadness dissipated with each bite.

Unfortunately, this bullying and binge eating of chocolates became a regular occurrence.

Next up, I'd just turned nineteen and went to visit my boyfriend at his home. I sat in his lounge room watching a movie whilst eating a block or two of chocolate. He was texting another girl, cheating on me. Young enough to believe that love would conquer all, I soon came to realise this wasn't the case and that he'd been cheating for a long time.

Eight weeks after giving birth to my first baby, I overheard one family member telling another that I'd gained weight and needed to do something about it because I was getting "fat."

Whether I was, or not, doesn't really matter; I was tired and completely exhausted, and you can only imagine my distress at hearing this while trying to cope with a newborn and post-natal depression.

By this stage, my binge eating had really kicked into gear. My feelings were out of control and I was incredibly unsure about what I was experiencing emotionally, and how to control the unwanted feelings of despair and sadness.

My fifth memory involves me taking 20-30 Panadol to try to end my life.

Looking back as an adult, I feel sorry for the child who felt alone and scared. Speaking up about eating disorders and mental health was not a big thing back in the 1980s. Bullying was, and unfortunately still is, a commonplace occurrence at schools, the effects of which were not recognised the way they are now.

As a child, expressing your feelings to an adult was hard because there was also the fear that it was your fault and they'd be disappointed in you. My parents knew none of what I was going through because I kept it well hidden, instead becoming a difficult child who lashed out at everyone and everything.

I was introverted and quiet in awkward situations, outspoken with my parents, and ate my feelings to hide my true self.

My Depression Hit a Real High!

Life went on and I grew into a young woman.

A woman who felt introverted, unsure of herself, and didn't know where she wanted to go in life. I moved from job to job, never feeling secure or confident within myself. I didn't tell anyone that I was suffering with depression or an eating disorder because it made me feel weak and vulnerable.

Meeting my wonderful husband at a young age of twenty-one and getting married six months later helped me to focus my attention elsewhere for a period of time. In the first decade of our marriage, we often moved home for my husband's career and I relied on him a lot as I struggled to cope with severe bouts of depression.

Like most people, I tried not to allow depression to affect my life, but my husband saw it. He was so supportive and sympathetic to my needs but, unfortunately, didn't truly understand the full extent of my feelings. This wasn't his fault; you can be sympathetic to someone's plight but, unless you experience what they are experiencing, it's hard to truly understand what and how they are feeling.

He's a patient, generous man who would, and still does, do anything for me, but he also felt lost because there was nothing he could do about my depression. He would listen, love me, and simply be there. I can honestly say if it was not for him, I might not be here today. I love you, Shane!

Unfortunately, my depression exacerbated my introverted personality, and my lack of confidence only became worse. I thought I hid it well, but I didn't. I thought people saw me as a snob who didn't like to socialise with others because I was better than them, yet this was so far from the truth. My lack of confidence influenced my choice to believe this was true, even though people did not see me like this.

Still, I would drag myself to gatherings with my husband, who was the life of the party, and wish people saw the true me, but they didn't because I never allowed it. Obviously, this also made it hard to make friends.

To make my life easier, I hid who I was and became who I thought people wanted me to be, so they'd like me and I didn't feel different to everyone else. I just wanted to be *normal*! Normal to me was being liked, being the 'fun' of the party, having people around who praised me and made me feel good. Unfortunately, I believed people considered me just mediocre!

Shane tried his hardest to boost me up by constantly telling me how amazing and wonderful I was, and that it wasn't me, it was them. If you've ever suffered with depression though, you know that nothing he said sank in and I never believed him.

The only time I felt good was when I ate, until I stopped eating, and then I felt so disappointed in myself for giving in to my urge to eat, for not being liked, and for saying stupid things.

My depression became worse, my feelings of self-worth deteriorated, and my binge eating became more frequent. My health started to suffer and, as life progressed, other health issues became apparent.

What Am I On This Earth For?

When I reached my forties, I started to really question what I wanted; you could say I was a late bloomer! I was working in jobs that were not my 'calling,' and I found myself questioning life a lot, and constantly asking my husband, *"What am I on this earth for?"*

By this stage, my binge eating and depression went hand in hand; if I was not hiding my bouts of depression, I was hiding my binge eating. Because I was not extremely overweight, I could easily hide my binge eating, so I felt that I was living life to the best of my ability. I was so wrong!

My bouts of depression were becoming more severe and frequent, and I was now also suffering from high blood pressure, sleep issues, and weight gain. The insecurities I had about my body topped off my lack of self-confidence. I asked myself, *What is the point of all this?*

Don't get me wrong, I had a wonderful, supportive husband and three beautiful young children. I also worked full time as a manager in retail. I felt as fulfilled as I could be, but still questioned what my purpose in life was. I wanted more!

I Could Say I Had an "AHA" Moment, But I Didn't!

I'd just started going to a new gym and being around women who seemed happy and fulfilled; little did I know the truth.

I listened to their conversations because I'd never felt confident to approach them, and standing on the sidelines seemed safer. These women were not happy! They looked happy; they sounded happy; their social media showed they were happy but, after listening to their open conversations at the gym, it was clear that they weren't.

They talked about their lives and how they were struggling with depression, anxiety, eating disorders, weight gain, emotional eating, fatigue, bloating, and body dysmorphia. They were coming to the gym to try to get away from these issues, but also to seek out support from other women who were experiencing the same.

I realised that I wasn't alone. These women were like me, hiding their true identities and faking it until they made it but, unfortunately they were not hiding it very well, just like me.

As a result of this realization, I wanted to do more to help women who were experiencing what I was going through, so I decided to study nutrition. So, no *"Aha"* moment where lighting strikes and I wake with a new lease on life. Nope, it was my need to help myself, but to also help women just like me who were hiding their true identities from the world.

So I entered a period of study whilst raising children and a husband (haha) and working full time, all while struggling with depression and an eating disorder. In addition, my husband and I were going through a financial shit storm and looking down the barrel of bankruptcy.

You can only imagine how that affected my depression and eating. I upped my anti-depressants and soldiered on, or so I thought.

Now, I am not telling you this for sympathy—the exact opposite, actually! I want you to see where my story of becoming a badass woman really started.

To say that I felt very tired and hard done by was an understatement, but I wanted to help these women so much that I did the whole "head down, bum up" thing, and completed my studies while trying to ignore the crap going on around me. You know, the whole *ignore it and it shall go away* trick? But nope, it was still there; the bankruptcy fight, depression, and stress of working full time while studying.

My husband and I made it through those tough times, but that's another story.

Flourish Nutrition & Health was Born, I was Re-born!

To say it was easy would be lying. I had this beautiful notion that I'd start my business and women would flock to my door wanting my help. This was not the case. I forgot that women don't like to admit when they need help. They don't reach out, and believe that being Superwomen is their only option.

Now, don't get me wrong, I really didn't feel I had much to offer these women except a listening ear, life experience, and a course I'd just completed. At this point, it didn't feel like much. So, I started working on myself, my friends, and my family members. I researched, asked questions, and was lucky enough to have friends in the field of health whose brains I could pick.

Over time, my confidence grew while, inversely, my depression decreased. I focused on my health a lot more, using mediation, eating to reduce inflammation throughout my body, and getting regular daily exercise. I was also seeing a great therapist.

The problem was that my binge eating was still in the background and I continued to hide it. It's also important to note that, until I started studying nutrition, it had never crossed my mind that I was binge eating. I was shocked to realize that I had all the traits of a binge eater. It blew my mind to discover that I was in so much denial.

I thought about how many other women hide emotional eating issues while putting out to everyone around them that nothing was wrong. I knew at this stage I had found my purpose in life, the one part of my mission that had been missing.

Over time, I'm happy to say my depression dissipated after many hours of therapy and, for six to eight years, I was in remission. Unfortunately, if you know anything about depression and anxiety, they go hand in hand. I discovered this four years ago when I started having panic attacks and was diagnosed with severe anxiety.

I'm not going to focus on what anxiety did to my life. I want to focus on how I got to the stage where having the anxiety no longer defines who I am. You see, after researching, picking people's brains, and being a guinea pig, I unexpectedly created a program to help women with emotional eating disorders.

I used my own eating issues to find out what worked for me and for other women. Nutrition is only one aspect of the program. It offers full support, guidance to lose weight, and the understanding to help rebuild self-confidence, which is why it works so well. Perfecting the program involved hours of delving into inner feelings, learning how foods affect the body, the aspects of sleep issues and bowel problems, how the mind controls our thoughts, and connecting with other women experiencing similar issues. I was on to a winner!

Winner, Winner, Chicken Dinner!

I started with one client at a time, kept improving my programs, creating new recipes (did I mention I'm a chef?), and making sure I got my clients across the line into a new, improved lifestyle. I started to truly flourish.

Now, don't get me wrong, my business was not thriving at this point as Covid had struck with a vehemence and impacted my business to the point where, for months, I had minimal clients. I never gave up and, even to this day, I won't.

I continue to always look to improve my business wherever possible. My clients always remain my first priority and their successes become my successes. To say that I love what I do would be BS because it's my *passion*.

I mentioned earlier that I was looking for my purpose and that, aside from my kids and husband (who are my life), my business is my calling. Helping women to see the strength they have buried inside and to help them acknowledge their importance in this world is why I'm here.

You see, women often struggle to acknowledge when they need help, and place a lot of importance on appearing strong. They hide the struggles they're having with eating, stress, anxiety, depression, and juggling so much in their daily lives.

This is where my program is so different. It not only focuses on learning how to eat delicious, nutrient-dense foods, but helps with sifting through the burdens of the mind which hold women back from being their true selves. I listen, sympathise, totally understand and teach them to live a lifestyle where they feel confident and in control, whilst showing them how to cook and eat healthy meals.

Don't Let Shit Get in The Way!

Currently, I'm working on a new IBS program, something very close to my heart. I'm forever trying to improve myself and the programs I offer my beautiful clients.

With the impact of stress on our minds and bodies, I know I'll always struggle with binge and emotional eating. I'll always have bouts of anxiety and the possibility of the return of depression. These are things I live with and that's ok. I don't feel weak or quiet anymore. I no longer question why I'm on this earth.

I still have a long way to go with building my business as, at four-years-old, it is still quite young. There are still days where I wonder if it's worth the sleepless nights, financial stress, and 24/7 support, but they are fleeting thoughts that dissipate pretty quickly when I think of my clients and their struggles.

I now see my emotional eating for what it is and don't allow it to control me. I'm confident within my business and what I offer my clients, and I know after having over a hundred successful clients, that my program helps others to achieve their health goals.

Life is tough, but embracing our true calling and who we really are helps us to understand what we're capable of. I couldn't have accomplished the things I have without the shit life has thrown at me, and that's ok because this has helped me to embrace who I truly am and made everything I've achieved possible.

My clients get the best of me and everything I've experienced makes me the person I am today!

I've found my true calling. I'm not quiet anymore. I *am* a Badass!

ABOUT SIMONE

 Simone James is the Founder of Flourish Nutrition & Health, a Chef, Nutritionist, and Women's Health Advocate. She champions her clients to achieve their health goals by teaching them to embody their true worth, release negative food behaviours, and learn how to remove the years of sabotaging diet myths.

Her passion for helping others stems back to over twenty years of constant weight and health issues. She is an Innovative Mentor who has created *Healthy Gut, Kick IBS,* and *Flourishing Weight* programs to nurture her clients who have tried everything to achieve their health goals. Her belief in her programs is unequivocal, as she offers her clients non-judgment and unlimited support; their achievements are at the forefront of her success.

Simone wants to change the world of "fad diets" so they no longer exist and nutrient-dense eating is the norm.

Simone lives in Ballarat, Australia, with her loving husband, three gorgeous kids, and two fur babies.

Connect with Simone:

14

TAMMY MANSFIELD

COMING HOME TO YOU

Epiphany!

It was a gorgeous, sunny Sunday morning at my local beach. A slight breeze in the air took the sting out of the sun as people and families sat scattered on the lawns and sand, and meandered the path on foot, bikes and scooters. New to the area, I decided to keep walking to see what was further along the beach path.

A happy and relaxed vibe filled the air as people greeted one another with a smile; I couldn't help but walk along smiling too, feeling so grateful, happy, and abundant that I could be part of this. As I stood on the boardwalk overlooking the water, I reflected on how much this experience aligned with my soul.

This made my heart smile and I felt a sense of freedom, which is one of my top five values. Finally, it hit me—I had the time, resources, and freedom to choose to do this with my time. I've always wanted, craved, and worked towards living my best life, being authentically me, and living true to my values.

Today I had hit that trifecta; I felt so alive, content, and happy all at the same time.

Life didn't start out that way for me. Like most of us, I faced obstacles as I was influenced, conditioned, forced, manipulated, and even coerced into being who others wanted me to be, or thought *they* had to be, so I, in turn, followed suit.

Not to mention that, as humans, we experience trauma of varying degrees from birth throughout our childhood and, in some belief systems, past-life trauma and pain, which can leave us with deficits and catching up to do as adults.

Early Experiences Shape You

My early childhood experiences shaped, influenced, and convinced me of who I was, where I fit into the world, and what I was capable of. These beginning limits that were placed on me, combined with simultaneously occurring events and experiences, created trauma that became part of my adult journey to recognise and heal.

Mum was a very loving woman who often said, *"You can do anything you put your mind to,"* and, *"Where there's a will, there's a way."* These two beliefs have served me well.

However, she also told me, *"No man will want you if you gallivant around,"* and many other things that implied I was not feminine enough to have a man accept me in a relationship.

Dad was a very opinionated and freedom-loving man who taught me to question everything and told me that I could do anything I desired as long as I was prepared to accept the consequences of my actions. He also raised me to be fiercely independent, which gave me confidence to give most things a go and to back myself, which was very helpful.

Unfortunately, even though I know my dad loved me, he was very closed-off emotionally and lacked the ability to give me the emotional connection and understanding that was crucial for a child to learn how to form healthy attachments. This left me with a couple of deficits.

I wanted him to see me as I truly was, not as he wanted to see or was striving to create in me, and I could never express my love in the ways that came naturally to me because I felt rejected and "silly" whenever I tried.

After our family broke down the year I turned ten-years-old, things only got worse for me emotionally because, as much as I knew my parents loved and provided for us, they lacked the skills to recognise their own emotions, ours as children, and the importance of nurturing that very much needed human aspect.

I entered the adult world at seventeen-years-old when I left home for the first time. Fiercely independent, moderately estranged from my family, and very angry and hurt—emotions I attempted to stuff down—I felt confident and capable enough to stand on my own two feet.

Unfortunately, I lacked emotional maturity and understanding, and was deeply afraid of the close connections I craved in my relationships; there was a hole in my soul.

I believe that our parents always do the best they can, and it's inevitable that we take on board most, if not all, of their beliefs, values, and way of life; it's human nature. One of our core needs as humans is to belong.

Unfortunately, this becomes problematic when we have to sacrifice too much of who we authentically are in order to feel like we belong and are loved. If all our developmental needs aren't met—in my case, healthy emotional and relational practices—or the process is interrupted, never quite addressed or repaired, this also becomes problematic.

We discover as adults that we can't quite achieve what we want for our lives, and may suffer debilitating emotions, physical ailments, and broken relationships—and may not even know why.

You Are Not Who They Told You

We manage the best we can. We only know what we know and we certainly don't know what we don't know!

Although I didn't realise it, I was depressed for the first ten years after I left home, but I was doing my best to live a "normal" life. I'd been raised with a great work ethic, was confident due to my fierce independence, and had excellent people and communication skills. Finding work, looking after myself, and connecting with people and resources to help me was no problem. In fact, all my life, I've been blessed to have excellent friends and have even felt a good sense of support from strangers who became my rocks in a very tumultuous world.

During my twenties, I was the joker, comedian, protector, and capable one. These were the masks I wore to cover how bad I felt inside; I helped everyone, ran to their side in an attempt to feel loved, and was an over-giver in every sense of the word. Yet I constantly felt not good enough or worthy to receive.

By the age of twenty-seven, and after two years of not really speaking to my parents, I had a breakdown.

My workmates dragged me to a local GP, where I became horrified as we discussed medication for depression. I'd been raised to be anti-pharmaceutical and self-reliant in my decision making, so being told I didn't know my own mind was a frightening experience. Fortunately, he was a good GP and convinced me that taking the medication was like using crutches for a broken leg—it was required only for as long as needed until my emotions and mind stabilised. He also mandated that I should see a psychologist for six weeks to help create some lifestyle changes. This was the best thing that could have happened to me.

The Universe was indeed looking out for me because after a brief rest at my Grandmother's, I became determined to understand all there was to know about depression, from what caused it to how I heal it.

Since leaving home, I'd unknowingly lived with depression caused by many unacknowledged childhood emotions. I'd had an abortion that nobody knew about, had found my pregnant best friend and housemate dead on our lounge room floor, and come close to suicide several times which, by the grace of God, I hadn't followed through on.

I'd had a few "not very nice" boyfriends and one excellent one, but it didn't work out with him because neither of us had the emotional or relational skills to handle growing conflict. We both brought our own childhood traumas into the relationship, not knowing that we could heal them, let alone how to.

If I had to sum myself up during those years, the saying, "I would rather be chucked into a tiger's cage than get close to any other human," would have been entirely accurate. Others may have gotten a giggle from this but, for me, it was absolutely serious. I was petrified of marriage and children, which I had initially wanted, based on what I'd witnessed growing up. Somehow, it was safer to shut my heart off, keep to myself emotionally, and focus on helping everyone else with their issues, trauma, and pain.

What I didn't realise was that this was the beginning of a true healing journey and the realisation that our past doesn't have to define our future. We get to co-create our life with the Universe.

From Surviving to THRIVING

What I've always wanted and tried to support others to do professionally and personally is to:

- Understand healthy emotional and mental health practices.

- Know that who we are is enough.

- Understand how we grew up, and that the past doesn't have to define the future.

- Know how we feel is normal and understandable, and our feelings and emotions have to be safely expressed and honoured.

With a combination of, and commitment to, the items below, we can truly change the course of our lives and create a life we love, based on what matters most to us:

- **Relationship with Self:** Prioritising this, and creating a healthy relationship, is the best investment you'll ever make for yourself, your children, partner, friends, community, and the world at large.

- **Mindset:** Be aware of your internal beliefs, thought patterns, and self-talk. Learn to reframe them from unhelpful to a place where they serve your Highest Good.

- **Energy:** Learn how your environment affects you and everything you see, hear, taste, and feel, and encompasses your physical and spiritual energy.

- **Emotions / Feelings:** Do the work to understand what they are, why we have them, and how we manage them. Your emotions are your friend, not the enemy!

I am certain everyone can relate to this on some level but, for the longest time, I felt weird, alienated, and like I didn't belong in this world. I desperately wanted to fit in and, even though I've always had a strong pull towards the spiritual, the unseen, crystals, flowing skirts, and hippyish attire and habits, I didn't allow myself to fully express this part of me. I felt restricted inside as I squashed and hid the full essence of who I am, because those I was closest to during those times were "different," and all I wanted was to fit in, which is perfectly understandable given that one of our core needs as a human is to "belong."

As we grow up, our family, parents, community, and culture are our world. We have a fundamental need to belong; as tiny babies and small children, we are dependent on our caregivers, believe everything we hear—as gospel, so the saying goes—and we are like tiny sponges who absorb our experiences.

Add to this the fact that children perceive the world very differently to adults. For example, as adults, you could jokingly say to your friend, *"How could you not know that? You're so silly!"* and your friend, if they have a healthy sense of worth, would probably laugh it off, shake their head, and giggle at themselves and their oversight or forgetfulness. If an adult says this to a child, however, the child may interpret this literally and take that on the belief that they are silly and lacking in intelligence. That's how easy it can be to contribute to low self-worth in a child.

When children bear witness to events, they can interpret them to mean something that makes them feel bad, and it doesn't even have to be a frightening event. This is why it's vital to instill as much emotional intelligence and understanding into our children as possible, so they feel comfortable to ask when they feel confused or frightened. When you build solid, close relationships with children, you can observe and inquire how they are going; it's quite common for children to express really heavy, frightening feelings in creative ways.

Most of us understand our moral code and the ethics that we live by, but even some of these beliefs are ones we have adopted from our parents, society, religion, and culture, and, in my humble opinion, should be up for close examination to see if they really work for us and for others?

One particular belief that comes to mind, that I've certainly changed over the years, is that we are responsible for another person's happiness, success, and emotions. I've tested this and experienced both ends of the spectrum and wholeheartedly agree that, if you choose to be a parent or caregiver of a child, then yes, it is your responsibility to teach the child how to flourish and learn to fill their own cup.

My personal take on our responsibility to others can be summed up in this quote by the Dalai Lama, "Our prime purpose in this life is to help others. And, if you can't help them, at least don't hurt them." I aspire to live by this new code. I enjoy helping others when and where I can, but I will not take on the guilt, obligation, or threats, both direct and subtle, that it's my responsibility to be there in every capacity somebody demands of me.

I'm a big fan of the teaching, "Give a man a fish, and you feed him for a day. Teach a man to fish, and you feed him for a lifetime."

It was during my years as a Youth Worker and Adult Disability Support Worker that I became aware of these concepts and tested these ideas to see what it means to truly help another person thrive.

The term "Bleeding Hearts" is often used to refer to people who work in the care industry, such as support and community workers, nurses, and aged care workers, because when we see, feel, hear, and observe people in need, it activates something within us to charge in, guns blazing, ready to help however we can. Very noble, perhaps, but the reality is that we burn out, become resentful, stop taking care of ourselves, and constantly live, breathe, and consume vicarious trauma from high-level exposure to another's traumas.

If we continue being "Bleeding Hearts," it can actually enable another to become dependent while we are simultaneously giving out energy we simply don't have; this is not an ideal way to exist.

The research into the "Circle of Security" explains it best and is a fabulous guide to what tiny humans need to grow into their healthy, full potential—a balance of doing things for ourselves combined with having the support from others, when needed.

Soul Happy

These days I mostly work on being "Soul Happy".

To me, being "Soul Happy" is what lights you up, fulfills you, energises you, is easy and joyful, makes you smile and laugh easily, and gives you warm, fuzzy butterflies in your stomach.

It's being aware of the thoughts, feelings, and activities that make life worthwhile and meaningful to us. We're all different and our experiences are unique. For example, I love the feeling of being at Health, Wellness, Holistic, and Psychic festivals and expos. Of connecting with people outdoors for picnics, barbeques, bushwalking, and community events.

Nature energises me - the beach, bush, grass, trees, flowers, sounds of the birds, and waterfalls. I love spending quality time with my loved ones, laughing, eating, having fun, and feeling warmth and connection. I adore quality conversations about what is possible in life; yes, we share our worries and woes, but then we look for solutions and give each other support.

I've learned that all of me is acceptable. As for whether others accept me, many don't! But some of the most "abnormal" traits, trends, and conversational topics I possess are the very reason some people love me the most!

When "down days" occur, I remind myself of all the good I've done in the world. I've always tried to live an honest, open life, and help where I can. My core work has been in support roles with those who have been the most hurt, abused, and victimised in life, and that isn't a small feat. The emotional pull, upheaval, vicarious trauma, sleepless nights, long hours, the verbal abuse I've copped, and the physical abuse I've been quick enough on my feet to avoid—being in tune enough to know when to talk an angry person down, is, in my humble opinion, a great contribution to humanity and the world.

Wishing You Well on Your Journey to Soul Happy

Thank you for allowing me to share my story and thank yourself for taking the time and giving back to you. I hope you've found something in these words that can help you.

Please know there is no "blame game" when we acknowledge that people and our past have caused situations of hurt and harm. The qualities of understanding, empathy, compassion, and forgiveness are vital for our own inner peace.

I can attest to the fact that I've improved and healed relationships with my family of origin, some extended family members, and friends as a result of my own inner work. Other relationships have fallen away due to differing values and lifestyles, and that's ok; the important thing for me has been to adopt the qualities I mentioned above.

I now run my own business, *Souls Guidance* where I assist others to rediscover their authentic selves and create a life they love through coaching, energy healing, and wellbeing. It is my new "soul happy" to support others in this way.

Please know there is a wealth of information out there. Your journey is your own to map out, and reaching out for the sources and support you need will be the best investment you'll ever make in yourself.

About Tammy

Tammy Mansfield is a qualified Coach, Youth Worker, Energy and Meditation Practitioner, and licensed Heal your Life workshop facilitator. Her business, Souls Guidance, is based on Tammy's passion and expertise in emotional healing, personal empowerment, and wellbeing.

After seventeen years working with children and teens in Australian Government Care and Adults in Disability, Tammy combines her professional skills, practical experience, and personal journey of healing through depression and two personal breakdowns, to assist her clients in achieving a state of self-love, healing, and empowerment.

Tammy exudes warmth, love, and joy, and provides the support and tools necessary for her clients to reconnect with their most authentic selves so they can create a life they love based on their values and what matters most to them.

Her passions include the safety and care of children, wellbeing, the environment, traveling, and humanity.

Connect with Tammy:

15

Tandaza Ntikinca

Every Dis-ease Is A Valuable Teacher

In 2014, when I started a new job, I had a dream so vivid that I should have known it was telling. I dreamt I was standing on the landing of an old, steep, rickety staircase, while the executive team that I was joining stood down below. It felt as if I had caught the dream at the tail end; each of the managers had already navigated the staircase, and I was the last one standing. The fear and anxiety that crippled my whole being was tangible even after I awoke. I vividly remember looking over the new colleagues standing below as they engaged each other in merry banter, so oblivious of my torment until a colleague, who I eventually grew fond of, came to my rescue, extending his arm as he helped me to descend.

Between 1996 and 2000, I acquired my Junior and Master's Degrees in Development Planning from the University of KwaZulu-Natal in the city of Durban, South Africa. I lost my *tata* (father) at the tender age of thirteen-years-old and was always cognisant that my *mama* (mother) was raising three children and holding down the fort. Despite being aware of her entrepreneurial nature, which propelled her to establish various businesses for as long as I could remember, I was always wary of adding unnecessary financial stress to her life. So, from day one at university, I was clear that I must complete my studies in the minimum stipulated time.

By February 2001, I had bagged myself a job as a development planning practitioner at a start-up development planning consultancy firm which operated from a delicately styled Victorian house in Musgrave, Durban. I loved the intimacy of a small team, the abundant moments of solitude as I researched and wrote client reports, and the travel involved as my boss and I often criss-crossed the province and country to visit various projects and clients. The problem, however, was that the pay was too low for a young lady with big dreams. My specific priorities were to pay off my student loans, then save to buy a car, and then a property. It was only in hindsight that I realised just how much my first job had been perfect for me in so many ways, especially for my introverted nature.

Recognising that our country was a new democracy at the time, I joined the public service where my skills were in high demand and the salary packages were far more lucrative. But I knew from the start that the public service was not for me. Even though I quickly climbed the corporate ladder, from middle management in my twenties to executive level by my mid-thirties, the roles I played did not inspire me. I loathed the administrative nature of my work responsibilities, when all I really wanted to do was to get my hands dirty researching, writing, and conceptualising appropriate development strategies. I envied the consulting teams that we appointed to undertake research work and found myself resenting drafting *Terms of Reference* documents for tenders and doing other menial administrative work.

It was so annoying to watch the posturing of colleagues who seemed more enchanted by their hefty titles rather than focusing their energies on the execution of their craft. I found it so distasteful to wake up early to drive to a meeting at a municipality, perhaps in the hinterland of the province, only to find that our hosts were the very ones who were late.

I hated knowing that all the exfoliants from world-renowned cosmetic houses could not absolve me from the responsibility I had to own for being part of management teams that, every year without fail, scurried to dodge under-expenditure of budgets allocated for service delivery to the neediest of communities.

There was something distasteful about attending *izimbizo* (large community gatherings) mid-week to find community members of all ages packed into marquees like sardines as they listened to speeches whilst eyeing the lunch packs, food parcels, and free t-shirts. I could not wrap my mind around how it was okay for us, as management and political leaders, to be happy with such overwhelming turnouts at events. Shouldn't we have been more concerned with why so many of our people, particularly in the economically active age brackets, were loitering with nothing better to do than to attend an *imbizo* on a Wednesday afternoon?

It pained me to witness how well-renowned consulting firms that commanded big slices of our budgets would so regularly deliver shoddy workmanship just because the client was the government. My almost two-year stint in the new job was not easy at all. Although I was still working within the same sector of development planning, it demanded far more engagement with construction sites than I was familiar with. Despite my team comprising technicians required for operations, I lacked the confidence and flair I had exuded in negotiating previous portfolios. I never quite found my place in that work environment, and felt as if I was operating in a sea of smoke and mirrors.

Since the early days of my career, my spirit was always on the prowl for studies that would ultimately lead me to work centred around my passions. Over the years, I had researched and toyed with studies along the lines of philosophy, psychology, interior decor, and creative writing, as well as the arena of alternative health, such as *Ayurveda*, Chinese medicine, naturopathy, reflexology, and Reiki.

My work laptops will attest to this; they always contained documents and folders where I recorded new words, phrases, recipes, or graphics of home interiors that I found as I browsed the net. My spirit always knew that my calling certainly lay beyond the jurisdiction of the world of development planning.

When I could not fall asleep after regularly taking up to four sleeping tablets a night, I thought it must be my stress and workload that kept me from my slumber. Finally, I decided to pay my doctor a visit and almost fell off my chair chuckling when she diagnosed me with depression. Me? Depression? Never! *How could it be?* I asked myself. I had always taken pride in being a girl who sported a glass-half-full type of lens.

But, during that two-week sick leave my doctor booked, I realised that, not only was I indeed depressed, I was grieving the loss of *tata wam* (my father) for the first time, twenty-five years later. After many years of running from this wound, I began to revisit my last conversations and engagements with *tata*, and shed stagnant tears that had been engorged for over two decades. Filled with dread, I pulled back the curtain in our lounge that Saturday morning of his funeral and saw the family huddled around his pearly blue coffin. I saw myself place my little hand on his icy forehead as I broke into tears while bidding him farewell.

I saw *makhulu wam* (my grandmother) grabbing me, pulling close to her chest saying, *"Khala mntan'am, kufanele ukhale ngutata wakho osishiyile"* (*"Cry my child, you must cry, it is your father that has left us"*). To this day, I vividly remember her words and the feeling of release that came with being given permission to just be, to express the anguish in my little heart. But, probably due to the midst of the storm I found myself in, and my innocence, I did not grasp the wisdom and power in her words. I have often wished I had held onto them much tighter.

The process of grieving is often a source of discomfort for both the ones grieving as well as those seeking to bring comfort, which brings an air of awkwardness and a sense of dis-ease. It seemed like everyone was unsure of what they should do or say to us. An awkward dance began to play out in my tribe, with the adults taking the lead and the kids following suit. In our immediate family, as the grieving four, we must have dealt with our pain and wiped our tears in private moments. I do not remember *mama* ever telling us just how much her heart was hurting. I certainly never heard her share her fears of finding herself being both a mother and father to us, her three children.

I don't remember hearing Lulu, my elder brother and the new man of the house, sharing the load he carried as he helped *mama* with all sorts of logistics for the funeral and supported her navigation of family politics. He was only sixteen years of age yet, on that day, he became a man—no consultation nor succession plan deliberated—he simply put on the yoke and did what he had to do.

I can't even begin to imagine how Lizzy, my younger sister, at the age of seven, could have expressed what she felt in her little heart. I remembered how, for many years that followed, *mama*, Lizzy and I would go to sleep huddled in the double bed in the main bedroom. We began to see subtle shifts in *mama* as she began to ease her way out of the firm disciplinarian she had always been and expressed a more humorous side. I guess she knew all too well that we no longer had our middleman to run to, whispering, *"Please tata, do talk to mama... no scolding us please, just for the duration of this vacation!"*

My adult body literally crashed as I was not only diagnosed with depression but also suffered from anxiety, insomnia, weight gain of ten kilograms, and chronic constipation. One night I lay on my back in bed, my eyes wide open until the crack of dawn, as I realised that the following day was the 6th of August—the twenty-fifth anniversary of the burial of my dear *tata*. My psychologist told me that it was not uncommon for grief to resurface on the anniversary of the death of a loved one, and this was certainly the greatest loss I have ever known. The moments of solitude presented by my sick leave, as well as visits to my psychologist, gave me the momentum to reflect on my life's journey.

I realised that depression was not new to me; it felt so similar to the energy that saw me withdraw from so many social and sporting activities at school after I lost *tata*, especially considering my love for jogging during my school-days. It became very clear that, whilst I had acquired junior and postgraduate degrees, held various senior management positions, and built up a wealth of work experience over the years, I always carried an energy of dis-ease into every boardroom.

With *mama* being a nurse by profession, I had always followed a relatively healthy diet, yet it dawned on me that my monthly grocery shopping list always included a box or two of laxatives because my body was simply unable to digest efficiently. I was reminded that my *tata* had also struggled with constipation, and that his remedy of choice was the regular consumption of Epsom Salts. Thankfully, I met a homoeopathic doctor who prescribed probiotics and other natural remedies that cured my constipation. Given *tata's* fatal diagnosis with colon cancer, she stressed that it was critical to have a colon assessment when I turned forty.

One day, a white male colleague commented, *"You look very different, I hardly recognised you!"* Flippantly, I responded, *"Well, you know how us black ladies are, always switching up our hairdos every other month!"* It was only later that day, when I recalled his non-responsive facial expression, it dawned on me that he was probably referring to my weight. Although my weight had always fluctuated over the years, that time it was at an all-time high. I have since recognised that there is always a direct correlation between the wound I am running away from and the spike in my bathroom scale.

January 2016 marked the beginning of a two-month resignation period at my workplace. Although I did not have a plan for the road that lay ahead, I was comforted by the words of the late American theologian, Howard Thurman, who said, "Don't ask yourself what the world needs. Ask what makes you come alive, and go do it. Because what the world needs is people who have come alive." Indeed, I felt that I was coming alive.

My journey into self-employment was certainly exploratory as I dabbled in running various businesses aligned with my interests and passions. With my love for home decor and passion for African-styled prints, it was a no-brainer that the first business I explored was sewing various home accessories such as cushions and bed throws.

I found a lady who gave me a refresher sewing course, then I started to design, make and sell these products. I loved the sense of adventure in looking for fabrics in stores, as well as the delight I experienced in my knack for combining unexpected textures, prints, and colors.

Aware that my ex-colleagues would probably deem activities such as selling my designs at local market stalls, as a "fall from grace," I relished and found delight in knowing that, for the first time in my life, I was doing exactly what my heart desired.

I also invested in various network marketing businesses in the travel, leisure, and health and wellness sectors—strictly those that lit my fire. It was new and exciting for me to work with men and women who had a palpable fire for their businesses.

I was fascinated by the fact that these entrepreneurs were often not highly educated, yet banked monthly cheques that would have taken me a couple of months to make, even as an executive manager.

Unfortunately, despite the thrill of doing work that lit me up, my bank savings dwindled quickly, and I wished I had not been so dismissive of my psychologist's advice to have at least six months' worth of salary saved prior to submitting my resignation letter.

Possibly as a result of reading *Meditations to Heal Your Life*, a book written by the late Louise Hay (a teacher of metaphysics), I googled something which led me to the *Heal Your Life (HYL) South Africa* website. I sent an email expressing interest in one of their workshops then, some weeks or months later, a lady who was the representative in my province called in response. She told me she was based in the city of Pietermaritzburg, where I was serendipitously due to be traveling the following week. I attended a workshop she hosted and, later, registered to formally train with the HYL Academy.

On the first morning of the workshop, we were given an opportunity to introduce ourselves and I could hardly utter the words; *"Hi, my name is Tandaza. I know I am at the right place at the right time,"* as a feeling of "homecoming" overwhelmed my senses. All elements of the curriculum resonated with me—various energy healing modalities such as affirmations, journaling, and meditation—and I was intrigued to learn that every dis-ease experienced in the body, from backache and skin conditions to cancer, are all messages that are psychosomatic in nature.

I could finally make sense of how my tendency to eat in secret, which later morphed into an eating disorder and years of fluctuating weight, had roots in a little girl's unexpressed anguish in losing her first love. Chronic constipation were her spirit's attempts to say, *"Little girl, it is time to put down the baggage you have been white-knuckling for so very long."* I couldn't wrap my mind around how spot on the content was as I stepped back and reflected on *tata's* life events and identified long-standing resentment that transpired some two or so years prior to his demise—for that is what cancer is an expression of.

I know for sure that our life journeys are like a great river flowing to the ocean; their course, direction, and momentum are preordained. When we stick to our course, we find that the terrain, vegetation, and environment are as we need them to be. When we re-engineer it, we stagnate and find boulders along the way. The little girl in me who had loved to read, paint, and bake treats for her family had always known that she was a creative spirit. Her anxiety would always flare up in boardrooms, for she knew she had deviated from her calling.

As we travel the course, we must experience each season to its fullness, for when we are too eager to escape winter, we cannot appreciate the shine of summertime. By running away from my wound for so many years, I also cut off the inner guidance provided by my desires and calling.

I have heard people say we are spiritual beings having a physical experience, but I like to take it a step further to say we are also having an experience of the mind. You see, every element of our physical experience (health and wellness of the body, nature of our relationships, even how much is in our bank accounts) all mirror the workings of mind and spirit.

I know for sure that one will never experience a shift in one's physical reality without making similar shifts in the other two spheres. I love being a teacher of metaphysics who shares with her clients that is so much more to the physical experience than what we see.

About Tandaza

Tandaza Ntikinca, the Creative Director of *Divine Body* and a teacher of metaphysics, is intrigued by how "dis-ease" in the body has its roots in the psychosomatic. Her career was molded by her own personal journey, when her body literally crashed in 2015 after struggling with massive weight gain, chronic constipation, and a diagnosis of depression and anxiety. As she began her journey of self-healing, Tandaza realized that her diseases had been her Inner Being's way of telling her to start to live an authentic life.

She left employment in February 2016, studied the Law of Attraction and trained with the *Heal Your Life Academy* (established by the late Louise Hay, a teacher of metaphysics). Tandaza loves teaching her clients that whatever problem that they may face, be it illness, financial, or relationship struggles, the answers always lie in a shift in mindset and energy healing.

Email: tandazan@icloud.com

16

TERI KATZENBERGER

PAINFULLY AND FAITHFULLY FREE

Badass—By Any Other Name, is NOT the Same

Growing up, my limited thinking always told me that a *badass* woman was a female who was hard, vulgar, mean, manly, and just plain rude. She was BAD; a person other females could not approach. Over the years, when women called themselves *badass* or used "that" term in their work, business names etc., I wondered, *Why did they want to refer to themselves that way? As BAD?*

After some self-reflection, I realized that my own "world view" of a *badass* woman was not at all what I had ever been taught, thought, and assumed. You see, I never really met a *badass* woman, only BAD women.

A *badass* woman is confident in who she is. It's not the kind of confidence that is all up in your face. It's not arrogant, intimidating, or a pretense of bravery. Her confidence is quiet and real. It comes naturally for her, and to her. A *badass* woman is confident in her ability and know-how. In her "Why." In understanding why she was created for this thing called life. And in her confident, courageous ability to be who God created her to be, regardless of who the world says she should be.

Allow me to introduce you to Polly, aka Teresa, aka Teri, *Up Close and Personal. My Real, Raw Truth.*

Invisibly Polly—Unapologetically Teri

My twin and I were born in January 1968, in South Dakota, during a Midwest Winter blizzard. True story! We were not planned. We were never accepted. We were "the twins who were born during a blizzard while my dad was out getting drunk with his parents, my grandparents." We were simply "the twins who ruined our mother's life and happiness."

You see, the day she found out she was pregnant with twins was the day she had planned to take her blonde-haired, blue-eyed son and daughter—her "Golden Children"—and finally, leave my dad. But when she found out she was pregnant, and with twins, she decided to stay. She CHOSE to stay. And her choice became our forever punishment.

For nine months in her womb through the fifty-plus years that followed, we were forever blamed for ruining her life. Making her miserable. We constantly reminded her of my father's parents. Looking at us made her cringe and her skin crawl. It was mostly me because I looked like my grandmother. She absolutely despised everything about me. My voice, face, hair, personality, openness, and boldness. ME.

Born weighing only three pounds, we were placed in an incubator, where I stayed for the next three weeks. My twin, able to break free from his incubator, was brought home earlier.

It was not until I was an adult that I learned my parents named me Polly when I was born, and that during the first three weeks of my life, I was called *"Baby Polly"* by all the hospital staff who cared for me. But, when my parents brought me home from the hospital, they changed my name to Teresa because my dad felt I would be teased my whole life, especially from family; *"Polly wanna cracker"* and so on.

What I've always found interesting is that, although they changed my name, I was never called Teresa by anyone other than a few teachers throughout my school years. All I have ever known is "Teri." "Teresa" was never a positive name in my household, so I grew up hating that name, that word. I often wondered why I was never known as Teresa.

I also wondered, *What about Polly? Who IS she? Who would SHE be? Is she me? Am I her?* I had an invisible identity that was changed, and then forgotten.

Is that why I have always felt invisible? Why my life has been one big fight? To be heard? To be seen? To be noticed? To find my place?

"Teri" grew up making her mother cringe; her skin crawled when she looked at me or when people mentioned that I looked like my grandmother. All I have ever known is that "Teri" is a burden. My mother was always angry and unhappy with me for no reason other than the fact I was alive. I was in her space and ruining her life. She has forever blamed me for being born. For being alive. That's all I know. If it were any different than that, I would never know. Actions plus words equal a thousand painful years.

I have often wondered how "Polly's" life would have been in that old house. *Would "Polly" have been loved? Noticed? Included? Would "Polly" be a ray of sunshine and joy to her mother? Or would she, too, be treated as an upsetting disappointment?*

School came easy for me because I enjoyed reading, studying, and homework. In high school, I received a scholarship to college but, instead of being happy for me, my family said nothing. The first time my mother paid me a compliment, it was 2006; the second time was 2019. I remember those dates because it was so rare for her to acknowledge me, let alone give me a compliment. She couldn't even do it as I stood in front of her on my wedding day, wearing her wedding dress.

Every waking moment, I strived for her approval. For her appreciation. For her recognition.

While I am certain I will die before I ever receive kindness from that woman, I must give recognition to her for giving life to me. For that, I will be forever grateful. You see, God had a purpose for my life and, in order for Him to fulfill His creation for my purpose, I had to be born.

I remember the day, time, and road I was on when I finally forgave my mother for her hatred towards me. When I finally forgave her for giving birth to me. When I was finally able to accept the fact that she will never have love in her heart for me. At that moment, a weight was lifted.

Sneaking out from a family gathering in tears, I was so hurt from the belittling verbal and mental abuse that I couldn't escape fast enough. Shaken and in tears, I drove down the winding road, asking out loud, *What the heck, Lord? What the heck? WHY? Why do they treat me so horribly? What have I done to them? What have I done to deserve their constant hatred and discontent towards me?* I have said a thousand times, times a thousand, that I love my family with all of my heart. I have always said, *"I love you,"* to their faces. What I would give to hear it back, yet I continue to say it, anyway. God so loved the World, He created me! My family will always mean the world to me. Regardless of their behavior, I continue to send hugs and kisses to all!

On that winding ride home, after crying out to the Lord, my Heavenly Father answered me. And He simply said this: *"Forgive them for they know NOT what they say. They know NOT how they make you feel. They know NOT what they do."* The exact moment I received God's word and repeated it out loud, forty-two years of pain, sadness, sorrow, and loneliness were removed. (Although, when I walked into my house and my husband, my "rock," said, *"How was everything?"* I did break down and cry.)

Over the years, I have had the opportunity to share God's Word with others who experience verbal, mental, and emotional abuse. People who experience unkindness, hatred, and discontent at the hands of others. The simple words that He spoke to me have changed so many lives; *"Forgive them, for they know NOT what they say. They know NOT how they make you feel. They know NOT what they do."* And walk away.

Fighting To Be Me

My life has always felt like a never-ending fight. "This Old House," our childhood home, was always loud and angry; I was constantly on the defense and protecting myself. A thousand times, times a thousand, I have said, *"I am just me. There is nothing wrong with me."*

When I was nineteen, I married a monster. We began dating when I was eighteen and he was twenty-three. Little did I know, my entire family thought our relationship was a joke and a mistake. But no-one said anything to me; I had no adult counsel. My parents never sat me down to talk about what I was about to do. I never knew of any strong objection. You see, my family talks behind my back, belittling, judging, and criticizing. To my face, they say nothing or they put on a smiling face and pretend they are there for me when, behind my back, they laugh, roll their eyes, and put me down.

My college scholarship? I almost forgot about that. Although it was such a big deal to me, it was insignificant to my mother. Sometime after I graduated high school, I tried to talk to my mother about enrolling in college. I was excited and proud of myself, but knew nothing about college life, so I asked my mom what I should take for classes. My mother replied, *"I don't know, Teri."* I continued to repeat that sentence, over and over, as I tried to have a conversation about my interest in college.

After repeatedly batting that ball back and forth, I finally said, *"Mom, I need help. I have no idea what I am doing. What should I take? What should I do?"* She replied, *"I don't know Teri, just take anything to use it!"* I never understood why I was always on the receiving end of her anger and disgust.

So, frustrated and disappointed, I drove myself to the college to learn more and enroll in my course, Business Administration with a minor in Marketing. Still effectively a child, I had no clue what I was doing. Many people would be surprised to know that I love marketing and advertising; I thoroughly enjoy watching commercials, reading advertisements, and marketing materials. But I sometimes wonder if "Polly" would have begun her career in the Marketing and Advertising industry? I wonder how she would have done in college?

Although I passed with a C+/B-, it was a constant fight. I struggled. I really, really struggled. I never felt more alone than I did during 1987-1991. I had no one to turn to. I had no one to talk to.

During this time, the world didn't know that I was married to a grossly abusive man. Innocent, kind, caring, heart-full-of-love Teri married one of the devil's men. I felt trapped and broken. Every day, he beat me down physically, mentally, emotionally, and verbally. He made me believe I was crazy. *"No one likes you. Your family hates you. People don't like listening to you. People don't like being around you. Our friends think you're weird. They hate your stories. They can't stand to be around you,"* the verbal abuse went on and on and on. To this day, I don't know what damaged me more—the hard, hurtful words or the physical abuse as he hit me, pulled my hair out of my head, and gave me black eyes.

I married a man who liked me drunk so he could rape me. If I passed out and he was in "the mood", he would have his way with me. That is one thing I could have taken to my grave. However, the monster was so ridden with sick guilt that, after one "incident," he finally confessed to me.

I became so sick with alcohol that I couldn't function sober and, at the same time, I began to battle a chronic eating disorder. My life was not my own. I hated everything about myself and my ugly life. Although I never thought about suicide, I often contemplated hurting myself enough to be admitted to the hospital because I wanted my family to see me and feel my pain. I never heard from them. They never called. Never asked me to come over. Never came to my home. I was living in a hell house. One thing was certain—I would die of alcoholism or from the eating disorder. Little did I know, I was slowly killing myself from the inside out.

Although I had a wonderful job and was doing well in my retail career, the sickness of my abusive home and struggle with alcohol soon came to haunt me at work. Long story short, I ended up in legal trouble. From 1989 to April 1991, I lived sick, scared, and deeply abused. I was in and out of jail with the final verdict of a two-to-four-year prison sentence hanging over my head.

Although, according to my Probation Officer, *"Teri makes friends in jail. People enjoy being around her,"* my mother was even more ashamed and embarrassed by me. Thankfully, by the grace of God and my wonderful Probation Officer, I never saw the inside of the prison. Jail? Yes! Prison? No! This man fought for me, stood by me, had my back, and stood up for me. In my entire life, he is the only person who has ever unconditionally been there for me. To this day, I remain forever grateful and thankful that God chose that person to be my PO; with anyone else, I would have spent two-to-four years in a women's prison. He gave me seven chances... I blew six of them, but that's another story!

Every day of my life in that house of hell, I prayed to God, *"If I make it through one more year, I promise I will leave."* I always made my promise, but I never left. I waited for my Savior to knock on the door and save me. Then, on April 4, 1991, that day finally came. I do wonder if "Polly" would have made it? Or would she have ended her life? Would she have ended the life of the monster to save herself? A thousand times, times a thousand, I said, *"He should give thanks every day that I was not a hair more sober for, if I was, it would not have hurt me one bit to spend the rest of my life in prison for killing him."*

From 1991 onwards, I was alone. I was lost and broken, but I was clean and sober. I was free from that hell house and the monster. I was finally free to be me! Or was I free to be "Polly"?

By the Grace of God, There Go I

Free to be me—Teri/Teresa/Polly—over the next thirty years, I had to learn how to live my life and how to just be me. I had to learn what this thing called life is all about. I have always felt there isn't much about me, or my life, that really matters to anyone. I know that isn't true, but it doesn't mean I don't "feel" it. It doesn't mean I don't "sense" it.

I am now married to an amazing man. We went to prom together in 1986 and had our second date in 1995 when we attended our Ten-Year School Reunion together. Tim is my saving grace, my knight in shining armor. He has an absolutely wonderful family who enjoy seeing me, being around me, and love me with all their hearts. In another twist, his dad and my grandpa (my mother's dad) worked together when my mother and her sisters were young girls. Small world! God's World!

The first time I went to rehab was on April 4, 1990. On the same date in 1991, I went to an extensive drug and alcohol treatment hospital. Why is that important? Because my life has always been directed by God's timing. April 4th is Tim's birthday! We married on May 6, 2000, five years to that day after we started dating. He is my "living" guardian angel.

It ain't easy being me. This thing called life has kicked my ass a time or two. Or three. Or four. The truth is, I was born a *badass*. I have kicked the devil around a thousand times, times a thousand. Regardless of hatred and discontent, regardless of being for me or against me, I refuse to quit. I refuse to give in. I refuse to give up. On me! On Polly! On you!

Maybe that is what my life has been about? The everyday fight or flight. Maybe, subconsciously, I have been fighting for Polly? I have never "felt" like anyone. I have never "felt' significant. I have never "felt" alive. I have never "felt" like I am truly visible in life. But, for fifty-plus years, I've continued to move forward, walking by faith and not by sight.

The Truth Be Known

I am a beautiful daughter of the Most High King! If the truth be known, I don't know how to give up on me and I am afraid to give up on God because he has a divine purpose for my life. In 2006, I stood in the parking lot of my business, *She's Shapin' Up—Fitness and Weight Management for Women*, turning a bracelet around on my wrist that said: "W.W.J.D?" As I verbally asked, *"What Would Jesus Do?"* God replied, *"He would walk in peace to love and serve His people."* And so, my life began again!

ABOUT TERI

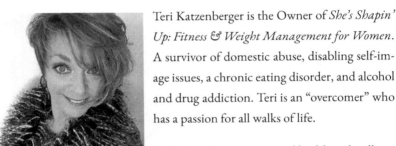

Teri Katzenberger is the Owner of *She's Shapin' Up: Fitness & Weight Management for Women*. A survivor of domestic abuse, disabling self-image issues, a chronic eating disorder, and alcohol and drug addiction. Teri is an "overcomer" who has a passion for all walks of life.

Beginning her own personal health and wellness journey in 1991, to save her own life, Teri has dedicated herself to helping women. Sharing everything she implements to live a healthy, well, fit, strong, and whole life makes Teri the perfect choice for women who want to stop the diet roller coaster and embrace sustainable changes, while learning to feel great about themselves.

Teri holds a diploma as a Fitness and Nutrition Specialist from Penn Foster University and a Medical Fitness diploma as a Hormone Fitness Specialist. Teri teaches women how to redesign their life—physically, emotionally, and spiritually.

Connect with Teri:

17

Trisha Trixie Hunter-Merrill

Not Today Cancer, Not Today

From the moment I heard similar words on a popular TV show, I knew that was my mantra. Every day I wake up and face death in the mirror. When I go to bed at night, I don't have a clue if I will wake up the next morning.

I'm not being morbid; I'm being honest and true.

I am a woman whose life is all about cancer. I have Stage 4 Metastatic Colorectal Cancer. In 2016, when I first found out I had cancer, I had two choices: fail and let cancer take over, or be a badass cancer warrior and take charge of my life!

I think you can tell which one I chose by the simple fact I am writing a chapter in a book about being a *badass*!

Little by little, I found that I needed to use my voice and speak my truth more and more. My circle went from my five closest friends to my eleven closest doctors. As many of us do when we're younger, I had a vision of what I thought my life would be. Because I led a hard life, I never thought I would live past the age of 25 but, once I did, I decided I had better get my life in order.

In some ways, I was ahead of the game.

My children were born in 1990 and 1991. By 2016, I had been married and divorced, then married and divorced again. In 1988, I traveled to England, France, Switzerland, Austria, Italy, and Germany, then to France, Amsterdam, and other parts of the Netherlands for a full month with my spouse when we thought I was in remission in 2018.

I had modeled for well-known fashion magazines when I briefly worked at a modeling agency in 1988, and then did pin-up modeling later in life for fun, contests, and to launch my apron business that I had successfully managed for five years, bootstrapping it on my own. As a Portfolio Entrepreneur, I had a few other side gigs like being the *Passive Expertise Princess* for the Pep Club, a way to learn and earn your passive income potential.

Along with a mindfulness business and other gigs, my biggest money-maker and the business that I was most known for was being a *Web and Social Media Strategist* for over thirty-plus years, which was inevitably useful when I became a *Toastmaster* in Colorado and earned my *Distinguished Toastmaster* (DTM) as well as a few other awards like Appreciation Awards, *Outstanding Toastmasters*, and the honor of being *Toastmaster of the Year*!

During my life, I have done a variety of other fun things! I've been a singer in a band and a backup keyboardist. I wasn't very good at the keyboard, so I quit that and moved onto other challenges, like trying drums and then finally learning the ukulele and performing with my teacher at a bar for a student performance.

One of the things I didn't have was a degree. My life was not together.

In my scattered mind at age twenty-five, I started frantically thinking, *I'd better get a degree. I'd better get my life together. I'd better move on. I'd better learn to become something!* I went to school at Long Beach City College in the late 90s when I was married to my second spouse and finally earned my Associate of Arts degree in Liberal Arts.

The list could go on and on. You see, my biological father died when I was ten-years-old and, thus, I learned early that life is short. You have to live every day like it is your last, because it could be.

I became everything I *__thought__* I wanted to be until I got cancer. Being diagnosed with cancer only solidified that thought and, little by little, I became the person I always wanted to be—myself.

Cancer taught me more than I could imagine.

It taught me that I can be quiet and a badass, and that I don't have to shout to get attention. It taught me that I can speak my truth without yelling it from the rooftop, and that I can live the life I desire on my terms, even though I still may need to jump through hoops for others (like my doctors) to live the life I desire.

What was my biggest *badass* moment, you ask? Hold on to your bootstraps. Here it comes...

During the Memorial Day weekend in 2021, I walked away from chemotherapy and conventional treatment. I had already completed twenty-six rounds and was exhausted from a life filled with surgeries, doctor visits, CT scans, PET Scans, MRIs, ultrasounds, surgeries, trips to the ER, and chemotherapy sessions.

It ruled my life.

I wanted more.

I wanted to live.

In the summer of 2021, the doctor gave me a life expectancy of one-to-two years, but he didn't know if I would live through the next five. As it was, he was surprised to see me still living! He said they didn't expect me to still be around at this point but, because I do alternative therapies, they can't really pinpoint the reason for my survival; all they have to go off of is the average outcome after a patient stops chemo.

I should have told him I'm not normal. Never have been, never will be.

Who knows how long I will be here on Earth? I've already exceeded expectations. More and more, my life became opportunities to become strong and badass, but there was a fine line that I knew I needed to balance.

After leaving all treatment in a badass moment, I became even more badass.

Determined to travel, I became the *Badass Cancer Travel Warrior* and embarked on my *"Wanderlust Cancer Journey."*

I decided to outfit my Fiat 500cc with a rack on top, a cargo hold, and an awning on the other side. I asked my husband if the car was 100% mine and if I could do whatever I wanted to it. He told me I could pretty much do what I wanted, but anything costly we would have to talk about. I couldn't pull a trailer because the Fiat can only pull 800lbs, and a small trailer is at least 850lbs. It would have been better if I had the money to build my own trailer.

Instead, adding the cargo hold and awning at least gave me a nice, shady place to sit while I stopped at KOA Campgrounds, or when I went to Faywood Hot Springs with my mother.

I won the *Coolest Campsite Award* at the *Reggae Fest* in Iowa, with my awning up, hippie tie-dyed scarves as back flaps, and sun protectors and stickers on the car. Of course, I had to have my small sound box playing reggae all night long while I lit incense and danced around my fire!

Months later, by the end of my travels, people were contacting me and telling me on social media and in person that I had honed in on something that many are not able to do even without cancer: to be soft *and* strong at the same time.

To me, this is what being a *Quiet and Badass Warrior* really means. Soft and strong. Wow! When my new friend I met in Sigourney, Iowa, told me this, I nearly fell off my bar stool. I felt so honored, I almost cried.

This journey of cancer is not easy.

Being told I was soft and strong was like the Universe telling me, *"You finally did it! You finally became the person you always wanted to be. You finally are the person you can look up to. You finally are the you that you have always hoped for, longed for, and searched for."* Just like in the *Wizard of Oz*, the answer was with me all the time. I just didn't know it.

To me, being soft and strong means being a badass.

Little did I know, it also meant being quiet and badass!

Being quiet and badass means fighting the fight that not many people want to do. It means getting up every day and staring death in the face and saying, *"Not today, cancer, not today! No, you don't get to win over me today, cancer! You don't get to win over my life!"*

It's not easy getting up every day and staring down death, but what choice do I have? To give up? No! That's not me! As many who know me will tell you, I am a lover and a fighter, and I'm not one who gives up easily.

I think that's why I'm still here. I am so ornery that I refuse to give up! My family used to say that about my great aunts and my mom, too. Maybe there is some truth to that. Maybe I'm just ornery enough to stick around this life.

I do what I do because I want to live the best life that I can. I fight so hard, though it is quietly and softly as I muster through this world of cancer, maneuvering, turning this way and that way, and making sure I stay inside my boat and don't fall out. That is part of the lesson. At least it is the lesson of life for me.

We don't always have to shout to get attention. We don't always have to yell and scream at the world. Sometimes, and most often, I have found we just need to be our true, authentic selves. You may think I am ostentatious and eccentric but, in reality, I think I'm just like everybody else. We're all just trying to get out of here alive, but none of us are really going to.

I realize speaking all the time isn't what I need to do. Maybe I need to step back and speak less and listen more. Maybe I need to learn more and gain more understanding of other people's cultures, what they're dealing with, and what they're going through. Maybe I just need to be a good person, the best human I can be. Maybe I can be a starfish saver and make a difference in people's lives.

I know that's pretty egocentric to say and to think, but is it wrong?

In *It's a Wonderful Life*, Clarence took George back and showed him all the little things he'd done that made a difference in the lives of other people. Who knows what might have happened if I was not there to help others, inspire their lives, or help them when they were in need?

I know a few people who might agree that I was able to help save them along the way but, in reality, it wasn't me. It was the God-given gifts I've been granted that helped me to be that person.

The struggles I went through that made me empathic enough to walk a mile in their shoes to see and know what that feels like. Maybe it's leaving a legacy of love so that when I'm gone, they'll remember me and all the good, silly and fun times—maybe even those hard times too—that helped them to learn, grow, and to be better people.

I know that we all have the capacity to be badass individuals; not just badass women, but badass people!

You don't show you're badass by standing on the top of a tower with a cape behind you. You don't show you're badass by shouting it to the wind. You don't show how to be a badass by screaming at others at the top of your voice! No. Badass truly comes from a hidden, quiet, underlying way of living, knowing that being soft and strong is what it's really all about.

It's a great way to be, and it's not a bad way to move about the world. I hope you can learn from my experiences, strength and my softness, whether you're fighting cancer or not, and that you will come out and be the quiet and badass person you were always meant to be! I know it's in you! I hope it for you as much as I hope it for me!

Much Love,

Trisha Trixie

To learn more about me, please check out my books:

- Days of Corn Tortillas (Kindle only) by Patricia Hunter

- Falling Into Fabulous: A Phoenix Rising on Amazon Trisha Trixie Hunter-Merrill (my alias) in Hardcover, Paperback, or Kindle

ABOUT TRISHA TRIXIE

"Trisha Trixie" Hunter-Merrill is the "Sprinkler of Fabulous." From portfolio entrepreneur for thirty-plus years, with a hustle or two on the side, she decided to leave it all behind to pursue a life of love.

Her mission and purpose in life are to help the world by being a positive influence, making a difference, being a good human and, above all, by sharing her divine healing presence she leaves a "Legacy of Love" wherever she goes.

Trisha Trixie is an Author, Inspirational Speaker (as well as a Distinguished Toastmaster), Freelance Cancer Model, Fashion Designer, Blogger, Influencer, and a MBSR Certified Practitioner! She has had the great joy of facilitating personal transformation for empaths and sensitive people since 2007.

Trisha Trixie offers her talents and gifts to help the world whenever and wherever possible.

She is... The One and Only Trisha Trixie!

Connect with Trisha Trixie:

Exclusive Book Bonuses

To download, scan the QR code, or visit:

https://sqr.co/qab-book-bonus

Made in United States
Orlando, FL
19 November 2022

24750968R00111